Marjorie Salisbury

A GARDENER'S LIFE

A GARDENER'S LIFE

The Dowager Marchioness of Salisbury

Photographs by Derry Moore

F

FRANCES LINCOLN LIMITED
PUBLISHERS

FOR MY DEAR CHILDREN,
ROBERT, RICHARD, CHARLES,
VALENTINE, ROSE, HENRY
AND MICHAEL

Frances Lincoln Limited
4 Torriano Mews
Torriano Avenue
London NW5 2RZ
www.franceslincoln.com

A Gardener's Life
Copyright © Frances Lincoln Limited
Text copyright
© The Dowager Marchioness of
Salisbury 2007
Photographs copyright
© Derry Moore 2007
except as listed on page 208
Drawings copyright
© The Dowager Marchioness of
Salisbury 2007
except as listed on page 208

British Library Cataloguing in
Publication Data
A catalogue record for this book is
available from the British Library.

ISBN 978-0-7112-2649-4

Designed by Becky Clarke
Printed and bound in China

9 8 7 6 5 4 3 2 1

CONTENTS

INTRODUCTION

When my publisher, John Nicoll of Frances Lincoln, asked me to write this book, while I was flattered to be asked, my first reaction was to say no immediately. My last book had recently been published – 28,500 words, nothing for a professional writer, who would have tossed it off in a twink, no doubt on a word processor. Not being a professional, and finding modern technology an impenetrable mystery – a lead pencil was my chosen writing instrument – I found the thought of producing 50,000 words in a year, so soon after completing one book, a daunting prospect. Two things made me change my mind and say yes. Firstly, I was touched and delighted that my designs for gardens were thought to be worth reproducing in a book and, secondly, Derry Moore was to take the photographs for it. He and I had collaborated on the book I had written in 1988 on the gardens of Queen Elizabeth The Queen Mother. Derry, as is widely known, is a superb photographer and it had been an enjoyable collaboration.

The gardens I have described here, and the designs I have done for them, were produced by a complete amateur. A two-week garden design course at the Royal Botanic Gardens, Kew, was the only formal work I undertook in an attempt to become more professional. I am not at all proud of this failure to achieve a proper training and the fact that it was more by light of nature than by study at schools of design that I was brought to the work of designing gardens, and more than once I have regretted the lack of a proper training. But that is how it has worked out, and I shall ever be grateful to my good clients who continue to trust me with their gardens.

Many things have influenced my ideas and ambitions to create the ideal garden. One of the most important has been the viewing of houses and gardens – looking, looking, looking, at Italian gardens, classical Roman gardens, gardens in Spain, America, Poland and Germany. Here, I feel, is the key to getting your eye in. Together with the houses they surround, many lessons can be learnt from these gardens about proportions and the relationship of the architecture with the countryside the building is set in, and about the plants and trees within them. If there are faults, you begin to recognize them: something is perhaps too high or too low for its setting, or an object appears somehow alien to a place, too big or too small, whether it is a growing thing or something made by a mason or sculptor. Occasionally there comes a magic moment when perfect peace descends on you, and you recognize that there is a total absence of disharmony between all the elements involved – the building, the character of the manmade gardens and that of the countryside around – and you know that this is the ideal you are striving to achieve in your work.

To try to create such perfection in designing a garden, you must learn other lessons, such as getting the feel of a place, absorbing its atmosphere, noting the setting, viewing the country around and, most importantly, studying the house within these surroundings, inside as well as outside, noting the views from its windows. Do they look to distant hills or downs, or flat farmed fields? Perhaps there are woods framing views, stately avenues, ponds or lakes; or the views may only be on to the surrounding garden, or gardens, great or small. Sometimes, of course, the setting for a garden can be a village or town, when very different things have to be taken into account, but nonetheless, some of the same rules will apply.

In setting out to learn about design, I studied drawings, plans and descriptions from the earliest times to the most modern. Few plans exist of very early gardens, but there are some mouth-watering descriptions of Egyptian, Greek and Roman ones, and many of the plants they used. One is Pliny the Younger's garden, where he sought simplicity and solitude, perhaps delighting in his lilies and his roses,

At my desk

for 'next to the Rose' he writes, 'There is not a fancier flower than the Lillie nor of greater estimation . . . and if a man should speak truly a Lillie growing among Roses becometh and beautifieth the place . . .' We can read Homer's description of Heinous' garden, and Virgil in the *Georgics* tells that Heinous' orchard 'various apples bears' as he writes of the 'Fruits of the Romans'. We can glimpse, too, gardens and plants in the murals in the ruins of some of the houses in Pompeii and Herculaneum. There is a beautiful reconstruction of a Roman villa that I have seen, with the only plants in its garden those grown in classical times in that city.

Visions of what medieval gardens were like can be found in illuminated manuscripts, and lessons can be learned about the charming intimacy of small, enclosed gardens. I found Gervase Markham's writings full of sympathetic ideas, enhanced by the delightful manner of his writing; and you feel he and his friend, William Lawson, could design a garden that would be admired and loved in any century, though the garden of today might be without 'the brood of nightingales' Lawson talks of as 'the one chief grace to adorn an orchard'.

After years of looking, researching and reading, I found myself entirely in sympathy with Reginald Blomfield's school of thought, which advocated a formal style, using architectural shape and structure with plants as decoration, and less with William Robinson's informal, naturalistic style. Are there exceptions? Perhaps. A house built in the eighteenth century, when the landscape movement was in full fashion, in a suitable parkland setting, is, of course, a pretty sight – well, a noble one, though I believe the most beautiful practical and pleasurable garden, in perfect harmony with the house it surrounds, is enclosed, a *hortus conclusus*: one that you can step directly into through your garden door, to be immediately enclosed by its sights, sounds and smells – delights that may also be savoured through your windows. From this garden you may emerge into a landscape, created by man or formed by nature, or indeed into a village or town street, for the enclosed garden can be accommodated in spaces large or small.

I did not neglect to read, study and, as far as was possible, view the ideas and creations of the great twentieth-century masters of garden design, such as Geoffrey Jellicoe and Russell Page, not to speak of those working today, for instance the Wirtzes, Kim Wilkie and Tom Stuart Smith. And I have tried to remember always Russell Page's advice to 'sketch, sketch, sketch'. This intensive looking, reading and researching, but above all looking, in an effort to tutor and train the eye, is not to imitate or copy but, by studying good design, to find the inspiration, to be inspired, to originate and to create, as far as is possible, something unique to oneself.

I am not good at delegating and I am sure I could never organize a large office, so I did not seriously consider employing even one assistant and therefore limited myself to six gardens at any one time. This was especially necessary as quite a few were out of England. I am grateful to my clients, several already friends when I started to work for them, the others strangers who have become friends; there can be few greater pleasures, at least for me, than to have a new garden or landscape to design. To have had six of my own (yes, I have counted my childhood gardens and the roof garden I am currently making at my house in London) to redevelop and design as well as the others described in this book has been the greatest of delights and good fortune.

In the Knot Garden at Cranborne Manor

CHILDHOOD GARDENS

From my earliest consciousness, I have noticed plants, although my very first memory had nothing to do with them. My first memory was feeling a rage of irritation because my sister's toes were sticking into my face. We were lying in a twin pram, head to tail as it were. She was nine months and five days older than me; I must have been about eighteen months of age. I loved my sister. We were not only near in age but later to share the same interests: drawing and painting, dogs and ponies, birds and butterflies, and above all, plants and flowers. This rage against her was unique; I never felt it again for the rest of her life.

She sometimes teased me, with no animosity, but strangely my first awareness of a plant was associated with her and terror. We were playing on the grass, and where the edges of the lawn joined the drive there were some plants growing which absolutely terrified me. I had been told they were dandelions, and whether my terror of them stemmed from their name I cannot remember, but unfortunately my sister noticed my fright and pursued me, carrying the leaves in her hand. I think she was not at all conscious of being cruel, not realizing for a moment how seriously frightened I was. Indeed, I was not cross with her, only very frightened. For her it was a game, a good tease. This strange phobia soon vanished, but it is odd that my very first awareness of a plant should have been associated with a disagreeable emotion and not with love and admiration.

That lawn is a vivid memory to me, not only because of the dandelions but because of the figure of the man who scythed it and the sounds that accompanied the movements of his tall body – at least it seemed tall to me, who could hardly have topped three feet. He wore canvas gaiters, a pale broad-brimmed hat, a neckerchief and a waistcoat over a shirt. I don't remember his face – it must have been cast down as he bent to the graceful movements of the scythe. He stopped every now and then to sharpen his tool, and the only sounds that could be heard were the gentle swish, swish, swish of the blade as it cleanly cut the grass and the harsher, sharper noise of whetstone meeting steel. I can see now the wet blade of his scythe and the vivid green of the grass lying along it, marking the lawn with narrow stripes where it fell from the razor edge of the blade.

Apart from the dandelion terror, I lived in a haze of content and discovery in that place. Called Boxley Abbey, it was not far from Maidstone in Kent. It was a house built in the reign of Queen Anne on the site of an ancient monastery, and an estate agent's description would certainly have mentioned its mellow rose-red brick, its walled garden and the romantic ruins of an old abbey.

Both the walled garden and these ruins were catalysts in changing my attitude to plants. They became no longer 'things' in my as yet tiny world, accepted as just being there, a part of life but of no special

At Castletown Cox with
my sister Ursula, my
grandmother and my aunt

individual interest. As my sisters (for now a second sister had been born) and I played about the fallen
stones of the abbey I noticed their vivid soft velvety mosses, golden and green with even an occasional
tiny cushion, brilliant like a cabochon emerald – not that I had ever seen such a thing or indeed heard
of it, but looking back to that picture, still lurking in my memory, that was what it looked like. The plants
that grew there took my fancy, too, creeping things. Our nanny sometimes had the country name for
them – bacon and eggs, Jack-in-the-pulpit. Jack had the face of our local vicar, whom I saw every
Sunday morning at the Matins service, although we small children were sometimes removed before he
climbed into his pulpit.

The piled stones, the remains of walls outlining perhaps chapel and rooms, were a place of shadows,
some cast by the trees that grew near by. I do not remember the sun shining there, but it was not a place
of fear; we children were entirely happy there, seeking and loving the treasures of moss and flowers we
had discovered in the caverns and crevices of this ruined house of God. Perhaps the earth was blessed
by the feet of holy men, whose lives of prayer and worship had left, like a lingering scent, an oasis of
beneficent tranquillity.

Another thing woke me up to plants: my mother's roses. She grew them in the walled garden and
took me with her on frequent visits there with basket and secateurs, explaining to me how and where
to cut a rose for a vase or how to prune roses so as to encourage them to flower again. The rose beds
were bordered by box hedges, and I can still smell the particular smell the box had when it warmed in
the sun.

My father was in the Navy and continually moved jobs from one naval station to another. My poor
mother moved house twenty-two times in twenty-three years. I do not think many young wives would

be willing to do that nowadays. She longed to be able to make a garden but had no possibility of doing so, living in short-term rented houses as she did. There was one house I remember well, because it was there that I was given my first packets of seed – Hook Cottage, it was called, a pretty, but plain, flint and stone square-faced house facing south. Of course, I did not recognize that its garden was a typical cottage garden, but when I look back now, I realize that that was what it was. I remember sweet peas and sunflowers, and my seeds had amongst them larkspur, godetia, nasturtium and, I think, cornflower. Oh, the joy of those seeds! I can see the packets now. They were white, with brilliantly coloured pictures of the flowers that I might see that very summer. The colours were quite unreal, of course, but how was a six-year-old to know that? Oddly enough, I do not remember the results of my sowings; perhaps the seeds never came up, but I have no remembrance of a feeling of disappointment or sorrow.

My third gardening experience in my childhood was a completely different one. I was older, probably eight or nine, and reading a great many books and writing verse, which I proudly thought was poetry. In those days children had to learn by heart – on Sunday before church – a verse of a hymn and the collect for the day, followed by the weekly learning and reciting of a serious poem by one of the great poets. Nothing frivolous or funny; Hilaire Belloc or Harry Graham would not pass the censor in the person of our governess. We did not mind. All we wanted was for lessons to be over as quickly as possible so that we could rush out to the fields and woods with my father's shooting dog, a black Labrador, Bruce, whom we adored and who adored us. I cannot remember which house this one was, of all the many my parents had, or what it looked like; only that it had a bookcase in it whose books gave me great delight, and where my love for books was born. I remember that it was spring and that the days were sunny. We had found a stream in a wood near by, and that stream is still fresh in my mind, the water clear, so clear that when we kneeled down and looked into its pools we could see the life in it: sticklebacks and minnows, darting water boatmen on its surface, caddis flies and tadpoles, and we even found a miller's thumb, a little fish with a broad and heavy head, the shape of a miller's thumb, which was said to become that shape from the miller rubbing grain between his fingers. The excitement of these discoveries! I can feel it now. We soon set up an aquarium in an old accumulator tank. A male stickleback was the terror of the tank, with his bright red throat and belly, and brilliant blue eyes. He guarded his wife fiercely in the nest he had built, threatening any other creature that ventured near.

But the greatest excitement of all was the plan to make a garden by the stream and build a woodland house. To this end we cut hazel wands and stakes and created something that looked somewhat like an igloo, the door just big and high enough, and the space inside just large enough, for us three children. UMP Cottage we called it, from the first letters of our names. Already there was something of a wild garden there, with primroses embedded in the banks of the stream, celandines, wood anemones and the dog violet, and we collected more and planted them there. Aubretia, a new discovery, was the only 'exotic' we moved there from the house garden and it did not look right. I remember disappointment. What pleasures there were in that house in the wood! It was hard to leave it, but more were to come when my parents, my father now retired from the Navy, moved to the West Country.

The prospect for us children of a first home that actually belonged to us was overwhelmingly exciting, as it must have been too for my parents, especially my mother, who would have a garden of her own for the first time in her married life. The house was in Dorset. It was the only piece left of a magnificent early Georgian house that had been the home of the Sheridan family, whose most famous scion was Richard Brinsley, author of *The School for Scandal* and other plays still able to entertain and amuse an audience today. The house was said to have a curse on it, the curse being that the eldest son would die before he was twenty-one. It had been laid on the head of the family a couple of hundred years earlier, when, legend said, he came across a poor peasant woman gathering sticks in the woods for her fire and, giving her a right ticking off for her thieving ways, told her to put them all back. My father knew about the curse, which had already fallen upon some unfortunate Sheridan sons more than once, but reckoned that as he only had three daughters he had no need to worry.

The house had several attractions for him. First, it was cheap; as he was an impoverished younger son, this was a vital consideration. And although the great house was gone, its setting remained. There were stables for the hunter my mother longed for, and for ponies for us, not to speak of the River Frome, which flowed at the bottom of the garden, with bullheads, minnows and sticklebacks, and trout too. The fishing was let, but I feel sure my father, ever an optimist, had visions of one day being offered a day's fishing; he had followed the sport with ardour all the days of his life.

However, he had a bad moment when he took with him, crossing the Atlantic in a forty-ton yacht, the Sheridan heir, Richard (called Dick), who was to have his twenty-first birthday during the voyage. His anxieties about this member of the crew were much increased because of Dick Sheridan's reputation as a bold, adventurous fellow: he had made something of a name for himself by sailing before the mast in one of the last grain ships to go to Australia, afterwards writing a book vividly describing his hair-raising adventures. Tall and very good-looking, and being surrounded by an aura of courage and adventure, he was an intensely romantic figure to a small girl of twelve. My father decided the only sensible thing to do was to batten Dick down below decks for the day and keep a sharp eye on him for the rest of the trip. My papa was greatly relieved when he was able to deliver him safely home. But alas, the ending of this story is a tragic one. On his return Dick went straight to North Africa to see his equally spirited sister, who if I remember rightly was doing a Lady Hester Stanhope in the desert, and there he died of blood poisoning after a botched appendix operation. Richard Sheridan's mother, Clare, was a first cousin of Winston Churchill, being the daughter of one of the two sisters of Jenny Jerome, who married Randolph Churchill. Dick seems to have shared much of his cousin's dash and courage.

I have wandered far from the subject I was meant to be writing about, but this romantic figure is part of a medley of memories of this time, encompassing primarily new discoveries to wonder at, hitherto beyond the bounds of my small world. My discovery of flowers and poetry and an intense delight in natural beauty resulted in attempts to paint and draw the objects of my admiration. The river drew us children to it more and more, with its water plants and plants that were lovers of damp and boggy places. In the water meadows that ran alongside stretches of the Frome were new plants to be discovered. I will always remember the excitement of finding in one drier meadow *Tulipa sylvestris*, the yellow wild tulip. My interest in wild flowers had not long begun and, arriving in this seeming paradise, I had quickly noted the woods and meadows, the riverbanks and even a glimpse of downland as diverse areas for wild-flower hunting. The future seemed full of promise.

But the present was exciting too. My mother gave my sisters and me a piece of land each to make a garden. The plots were tiny, probably measuring no more than fourteen feet by eight feet, but mine seemed ample to me and I set to at once to lay it out. The details of the design have been erased from my mind by time but I remember a narrow, rather wandering path, which went from bottom to top, where I made a pond. I did not know that a pond lined with clay would hold water, but I found a piece of looking glass which did the trick, and it supported a floating celluloid swan.

I was entirely satisfied with the layout of my first garden and promptly began to plant it, outlining the pond with small rocks and determining to go in for alpines. I had seen an advertisement, perhaps in one of my mother's gardening magazines, from an alpine plant nursery and my sisters and I wrote for its catalogue. This provided hours of pleasure, as we read the descriptions of the plants and tried to choose. The agony of decision! There was such a choice and our pocket money was limited – if I remember right there was a capriciousness about its arrival and I cannot really remember having any at all. Later we were to have Post Office Savings Bank books, but that was in the future, and great hopes were always pinned on godparents and their visits much hoped for and eagerly awaited. I was, with an exception or two, fond of my godparents, but I must admit that, at this moment of dour penury coupled with my longing for plants, affection was coloured with a mercenary tinge. They were usually good for at least half a crown and, I'm ashamed to say, I remember a certain disappointment when nothing was slipped into my palm.

Remembering the intense pleasure of making that garden, I also remember it never being a healthy burgeoning place full of colour. I do not believe I was a good gardener. I fussed and fiddled with the plants too much. I think I loved them to death. My growing passion for wild flowers gradually took my time away from the garden plot. Three years I spent learning about them, hunting for them and drawing them, while painting my discoveries in my Bentham and Holker wild-flower book with its black and white illustrations of British wild flowers. This, along with bird watching and butterfly collecting, was all-absorbing.

My sisters and I built up a considerable collection of eggs as well as butterflies, but we quite soon sickened of the last. We found the butterflies' eggs, and we watched them hatch and turn into caterpillars and then chrysalises and finally butterflies. I remember the wonder I felt as I looked at these diverse creatures, the quiet mole colours of fritillaries and meadow browns, the soft yellows of brimstones and the startling richness of the red admiral and peacock. But these beauties, and others caught in our nets, were then chloroformed and pinned to a board. This last operation was what brought the butterfly collection to an end, although quite illogically we continued collecting birds' eggs. In those times, few birds whose nests we could have found were rare, but when we stuck a needle into the fat end of the egg, there was sometimes a baby bird inside, in spite of us carefully putting the eggs in a basin to sink if fresh and float if incubated. The killing of these little creatures, with their stomachs bloated and transparent with fluff on their heads and signs of feathers, like the killing of butterflies brought our egg collecting to an end.

I joined the Wild Flower Society and was put into a group. My group had a lovely man who ran it called the Reverend Salmon. I never met him, but I know he was a lovely man from the letters he wrote me. These were about the plants I sent him, or descriptions of them. Great botanist as I feel sure he was, he wrote with humble courtesy, letting me down gently if my rarity turned out to be as common as a buttercup. Writing of him now makes me remember a verse from one of Hilaire Belloc's poems:

On my father's shoulders, searching for a wild flower on the cliffs at Killarney

Of Courtesy, it is much less
Than Courage of Heart or Holiness,
Yet in my walks it seems to me
That the grace of God is in Courtesy.

Every spring he set the group a competition. We had to see how many plants we could find in flower on 1 March. At crack of dawn, I was away on my bicycle, scouring the woods and meadows, roadsides and banks. I do not remember lunching that day but I do remember winning the competition. At the end of the year, you sent the diary the society gave you on becoming a member to the Reverend Salmon, with the finds you had made during those twelve months neatly written in, each with the place and date of its discovery. Back the diary came by the New Year, with the holy man's comments and criticisms in an accompanying letter.

Apart from Dorset, my Mecca for wild flower hunting was Ireland, my father's home and a country where I spent a great deal of my childhood. In County Clare there was the Burren to be explored – an extraordinary place, where stone replaced grass and rare plants found cool runs for their roots. Approaching the Black Head, you pass the Cliffs of Moher, their dark majestic walls holding back the Atlantic Ocean, the grass either side of the narrow road (it was 1935) blue with spring gentian. You could see the sheets of blue many yards away, so thick were the little plants growing cheek by jowl in the sward. I wonder if I am the last person alive to remember this amazing sight. On a visit twenty years or so later, it needed a considerable hunt to find one.

Lake Inchiquin was home to starwort, as it was rather charmingly called, as well as mouse-eared chickweed. There was an island in the lake, which in the time of Brian Boru was the home of my Irish ancestors. Many romantic legends are attached to this island.

Kerry was a rich field for wild flowers. My family had a cottage by the sea there, and in one spot, only on its land, there grew a plant called *Simithis planifolia*, native to the extremes of north-west Africa and south-west Europe. How on earth did it get to Kerry? Could it have come from a ship of the Spanish Armada, which Lord Burghley, Queen Elizabeth I's Chief Minister, noted in his diary (preserved in the archives at Hatfield) was 'forced into ye North seas and so with Great wrack passed homewards about Scotland and Irland'? My Irish aunt used to say the dark looks of many a west-coast Irishman came from sixteenth-century ancestors who had survived from the wrecked ships of the Armada. The only other

With my sister
Pamela at Dunraven
Castle, my
grandparents' home
in Wales

known site of this plant is near Bournemouth, and perhaps it is not too fanciful to think its seed too
could have been brought by a ship.

Memories of my childhood absorption in nature, and more especially wild flowers and gardens, made
me prick up my ears the other day when I read a piece in a newspaper. The writer was analysing
Wordsworth's ode 'Intimations of Immortality from Recollections of Early Childhood'. The poet believes
that our soul at birth comes with a memory of a before-birth existence: 'not in utter nakedness, / But
trailing clouds of glory do we come / From God, who is our home'. 'Heaven', the critic said, 'is about us
in our infancy but Wordsworth claims as man ages the glory dies away and will "fade into the light of
common day".' He denied that this happens to man, evidencing his own increased delight in nature each
returning spring. Comparing these feelings to his childhood lack of any interest in the beauties of
nature, and doubting that many (or any) children had the sense that the poet claimed for them, he gave
as examples to back up his view children 'yanking off the heads of wild flowers and swinging from the
branches of trees'.

I took issue with the writer over both these examples of a child's insensibility. Did they not illustrate
more a child's ignorance of how to pick a flower, rather than insensitivity to its beauty? The small fat
hands unable to break the often tough stems, greed perhaps already showing itself in wanting to possess
the beauty of cowslips, buttercups or lady's smocks, but surely not insensitivity? That would mean
ignoring them.

I remember the pain when tugging the stems resulted in a few headless stalks and stemless flower
heads left in one's chubby hand, and a feeling of a somewhat sad and guilty disappointment. Our elders
had said that without water they would die, so they were urgently but clumsily stuffed into a jam pot.
If thought and care for them had been absent, they would have been flung on the ground. But what

Picking daffodils at
Dunraven, with Ursula

about children swinging from the branches of trees and the sight convincing you that they must be 'less sensitive than apes'? My sisters and I, with a pack of cousins, indulged in climbing trees, one of the greatest pleasures of childhood. My Irish grandfather and my English grandfather were both dendrologists, in whose homes we spent a great deal of time, and although we were much indulged by them, it is certain that tree climbing would have been forbidden if we had done their precious trees any harm. Perhaps my sisters and I were eccentric in not conforming to the usual patterns of childhood, but I hope that we were not the exceptions that proved the rule.

My eldest sister and I were now sixteen and fifteen. She had been sent to Paris to be given a final polishing up before being launched as a debutante. The Dorset house was sold, enabling my parents to rent a house in London and give her a proper season, which was the normal thing to do at that time, continuing a tradition long established. So the story of the gardens of my childhood comes to an end. Naïve and simple as they were, they shared these characteristics with the wild flowers, and along with the flowers were the inspiration for my passion for plants and gardens, which has continued into my old age.

THE LODGE HOUSE

HATFIELD, HERTFORDSHIRE

The Marquess and Marchioness of Salisbury

The Lodge House at Hatfield House in Hertfordshire has always been inextricably connected in my mind with a legendary figure in my husband's family: someone with a character and personality so strong and vivid, so eccentric, funny and lovable, that even those who had met her only once never forgot her. I knew many of her nieces and nephews, three brothers, cousins and friends, but to my eternal regret I never knew her. She died only three months before I became engaged to her great-nephew. He, of course, loved and was amused by her, as all were, and one of the first things we did when he drove me down to meet his grandparents at Hatfield was to take me to visit his great-aunt Gwendolen's house in the park.

Lady Gwendolen Cecil (known in the family as T.T.) was the youngest daughter of the 3rd Marquess of Salisbury (three times Queen Victoria's Prime Minister) and his biographer, although she never completed the book and remained conscience-stricken about her failure to do so. She and her elder sister were known as the 'Salisbury plains'. Gwendolen's appearance was her character, a niece wrote, the dishevelled hair, the arched gravity of the brow, the sombre eyes and the straight nose contradicting the kindly but badly shaped mouth and, above all, the long clever hands which epitomized her grace and delicacy of mind. The same niece hazarded that a collect from *The Book of Common Prayer* must have been her constant endeavour: 'For as much as without Thee, we are not able to please Thee; mercifully grant that Thy Holy Spirit may in all things direct and rule our hearts.' Formidably intelligent and deeply religious, she was saint and scholar, her humbleness of mind running like a gold thread through her whole being and affecting all her thought and actions. I have written more fully about Lady Gwendolen than I might have largely because her house and garden were to become my first home as a married woman.

What was especially noticeable about the house was not only its simple beauty – it was set in a clearing of bracken and ancient oak trees and looked like a dwelling in a children's fairy tale – but that it had an atmosphere which must have been created by her saintly personality. She had lived there from 1909 until her death in 1945 – thirty-six years. The interior had suffered much from the neglect of the war years and, I suspect, lack of attention from Lady Gwendolen before the war, when she would have been in her late seventies and eighties. Her own comfort and appearance were not of prime importance to her (a niece remembers her wearing a battered hat decorated with a piece of unfinished knitting), and nor, I think, was interior decoration. An example was the dining room, part panelled in charming pale oak, which must have been very early, almost certainly seventeenth century or earlier; she had new panelling made to fill in where the original was missing, but it did not match the old, although clearly it was intended to. The main staircase was a beauty and unexpectedly grand for a small cottagey house. It must have been introduced in the mid-seventeenth century and lent an air of sophistication to the rather humble lodge.

Her closeness to the family at the 'big house' and its proximity to the lodge meant she was constantly visiting them and they her. The Prime Minister never expected his children to leave home, however old they were, but he had been dead for six years; otherwise she most surely would have stayed with him. Her youngest brother stayed at Hatfield until he became Provost of Eton; and when Lord Robert, another son, founder of the League of Nations, and his wife told his father they would like to move to a house of their own, although astonished, he saw the point and was very understanding.

I have wondered why she did not marry. Although plain, she must have had immense charm as well as being intensely lovable. Few could match her intellect, and she was passionately interested in other people and what made them tick, while being so humble and thinking everyone better than herself. I was told as a young bride that the family thought she might have married the Duke of Norfolk but was constrained by religious considerations, he being a Roman Catholic. It seems that he shared some of her characteristics. A guest arriving to stay at Arundel Castle passed a figure on the drive, shabby and dishevelled, a labourer, he assumed. On being ushered into the drawing room, the guest was astonished to be greeted by the same figure – it was the Duke. Lady Gwendolen was staying in the house and that night, her opening gambit to her neighbour at dinner was 'Do you soak or soap?' She was unusual.

There was a keeper's lodge in the Home Park at Hatfield in Tudor times, if not earlier. A survey of the manor of Hatfield dated 1551 mentions 'one little park . . . well fenced, set with great trees of oak, wherein are thirty four deer . . . and one lodge well repaired'. It is not known whether this Tudor lodge stood on the same site as the present Lodge House, but the earliest maps, dating from about 1608, show the lodge where it is now, and we know from references in the Hatfield accounts that Robert Cecil, the builder of the house and first minister of Elizabeth I and James I, built a lodge at this time. In the middle of the seventeenth century, the lodge appears to have been demolished and rebuilt for the 2nd Earl of Salisbury's third son. The records of its re-building make no mention of a garden – only that there was a garden wall of brick and two gate piers, very possibly the ones that are there now. References suggest that the place was 'like a small farm with a barn, a brew house, a hen house' and even a 'ferret' house. In 1657, the keepership of the Home Park 'together with the Lodge House' was granted by the 2nd Earl to his son for life 'to inhabit and dwell in with his wife and family and the feeding of twelve cows, one bull and five horses'. There are no references to the Lodge House throughout the eighteenth century, but there are a couple of maps that show that there was a walled garden to the south of the house on the same site as the present one. It seems always to have been the ranger's or keeper's house.

When we lived at the Lodge House there was a deer larder, where the deer that were shot were hung. This was a pretty, long low building, probably built at the same date as the present lodge, but it could have been earlier, and it lay opposite the lodge on its northern side. We turned it into nurseries for our children – four of our sons were born during the six and a half years we lived there – and very nice ones they made. A mischievous great-uncle of my husband's, the Duke of St Albans, essayed to be deeply shocked and had great fun telling the family and friends I had housed my children in a deer larder.

In the mid-nineteenth century, two families, the head keeper with wife and five children and a schoolmistress, and the family of the clerk of the works, lived in the Lodge House. It must have been a fearful squash, because to this day there are only five bedrooms and three minute attic rooms, but the house continued to be shared by two families for the rest of the nineteenth century. I suppose the walled garden, too, was divided and no doubt it was planted with the typical cottage garden vegetables, flowers and herbs.

By 1910, a new keeper's lodge had been built and in 1907–8 a plan was marked up by Lady Gwendolen with many proposed alterations to the Lodge House, showing that it was being prepared for her use, and indeed in 1909 her tenancy began.

My husband's grandparents proposed that we should live there, and what could have been a more alluring prospect? But there were several hurdles to jump before we could move in. The war had only just ended and wartime restrictions of many kinds were still in force, especially in the field of house building and alterations to buildings. The amount we were allowed to spend on the house was tiny: if I remember right, well under £300. The rules were extremely strict and there was no question of negotiation. But worse was to come. When the final bill came in from the clerk of the works for the pathetic amount of work that had been done, it exceeded the allowance. My grandfather-in-law, the most upright of men, was horrified and felt the only way, if there was a way at all, to atone for breaking the law was to confess the amount of the overspend – I remember it as being a modest sum – and offer the house to the council, which he did. Our hearts sank. The vision of our first home had vanished.

The box parterre

The councillors, stunned and stumped as to what to do, finally wrote to Lord Salisbury suggesting a compromise: my husband, a demobilized soldier who had fought throughout the war, was as entitled as anyone else to have somewhere to live and, provided we divided the house and put another couple in one half, we could have the other. Well, it was a good deal better than nothing.

We found a couple who wanted accommodation and a job, but alas, they turned out, though harmless, to be quite without any skills. We hoped the husband might do odd jobs and a bit of gardening, but he knew as much about gardening as I did about fish-life at the bottom of the Atlantic, and his wife did not want to do anything. When our first child arrived there was little room and I wondered where in the 1830s the head keeper had put his five children – they must have been head to tail in one bed. Our kitchen was in the hall and the washing up was done in a small washbasin in the downstairs loo. My husband took this on. He was a large man and a meticulous washer up, and it was a miracle that the china survived. I did the cooking. It was no pleasure, as butter, sugar and meat were still rationed and fresh eggs mostly a distant memory.

This rather insalubrious time finally passed. The couple left and we were allowed to occupy the whole house, so I was able to turn my attention to the garden. Lady Gwendolen's gardener lived in a cottage which she had built to her own design. Amongst all her other talents she was a very competent architect and had designed and built estate cottages both at Cranborne Manor in Dorset, the Cecils' other family home, and at Hatfield, and even a block of flats for poor old ladies. They were practical, but aesthetically not very pleasing. Every detail was carefully thought out, but the proportions always seemed a bit askew. This was to be wondered at, when she must have been familiar with so many exquisite buildings since early childhood; you would have thought her eye would have been trained to recognize how much perfect proportions contribute to beauty. It can have only been because her first concern was always for the comfort of those who lived in the cottage.

The gardener, Mr Norris, had been with Lady Gwendolen for many years – I forget how many. He seemed very old; he probably wasn't, but I was a young woman. He was large and rather fat and moved slowly, but he was a good gardener. Like all old gardeners, he did not like innovation. He liked to go on doing what he had always done, and he did it very well, but any suggestion of change in the garden was met with silent disapproval, probably largely because of his devotion to Lady Gwendolen. I hardly wanted to change anything, so our relationship was a happy one, though I had to screw myself up when I had to tell him the bad news that I wanted to add or subtract something. He always accepted it but made me feel a bit of a brute.

The garden Lady Gwendolen had designed was a truly delightful and imaginative one, and it was one of the things she loved best. Her niece said, 'We used to rush up to Aunt T.T. and say to her "go on about your garden!"' The same niece wrote, 'She always found out the best in people; she inspired them, and derived wisdom from them.' An example of this was her compassionate act in employing a man with advanced tuberculosis to help make her garden at the Lodge House. He was nearly a genius and loved his work. Together they designed, in a rectangle of less than half an acre, a garden of unusual charm and comprising almost every aspect of gardening. He knew what to grow and where. She developed the design. Norris must have done the physical work, as she could not do it and the sick man could only direct, when he was well enough. One can imagine what joy it gave this practically unemployable man to exercise his vocation and what joy it gave her to be the means to it.

Between them they made a rose garden, because as she used to say, 'A rose is the most completely satisfying flower.' A special corner was kept for Madonna lilies where they could be seen from the windows because of 'the special purity and whiteness of their corollas'. There was a pergola, an arbour to have tea in, a romantic hidden garden to be alone in.

She made on the west side of the house a small garden enclosed by a holly hedge, laid out with bricks enclosing small beds, and she planted here, against the low wall, a liquidambar tree. This wall surrounded the whole garden and is still there. It is built of brick and quantities of flint with a capping of tiles, slates and cement. It is rather prone to collapsing in places from time to time, but it is very charming; typical of walls seen locally in Hertfordshire, and suits well the house it surrounds.

Lady Gwendolen was a genius in the way she made this very small garden seem like a large one. She divided it up into sections by high or low hedges. She planted four cockspur thorns (*Crataegus persimilis* 'Prunifolia') in a square. They were standards and she clipped the heads in a square too; and she laid a brick pattern under them to keep your feet comfortable when you sat on the wooden seat beneath the canopy of thorns. They had beautiful, fat red fruits in the autumn and white flowers in May. She made a raised walk laid with slates and backed to halfway by a low yew hedge. The pergola had brick pillars and rustic poles connecting them, laid from top to top. I particularly remember a rose called 'Mme Alfred Carrière', its white flowers touched with pink and fresh green foliage. It is growing on the same pillar today, strong and flourishing. Lady Gwendolen chose well, and Mme Alfred is not the only rose from her time still living, robust as she herself was.

The hedges, raised walk and large pieces of topiary, randomly clipped, created a garden you could not see all at once. That was her genius. The whole garden was tiny, but because of the parts that you could not see, it gave the illusion of being much bigger. You were allured to explore what went on behind that lump of yew. If you went up those steps, what would you see? If you went down those others, would there be another surprise?

When in 1946 we came to live in the Lodge House, it seemed at first sight that there was little to improve in the garden. This was rather disappointing to someone who was eagerly looking forward to getting going with spade, trowel, catalogues and secateurs. But after a few weeks of contemplation, it became clear that there were quite a few things that could be done, although I was far from confident that I should attempt to be anything more than custodian of Lady Gwendolen's creation.

Five years of war and post-war neglect prodded me into repairing the damage. In some parts, brick paths had to be re-laid, broken Italian terracotta pots replaced, overgrown shrubs and hedges pruned and tidied. This was a start, and gradually, more and more, I got drawn into what I thought would be improvements, especially with the plants. The rose garden looked a little stark and bare. It only had Hybrid Teas. They were mostly pretty ones, but they seemed a little out of character with the ancient house. First I planted a box (*Buxus sempervirens*) hedge around the whole square of the rose garden, which seemed to help take its starkness away. The roses had no other plants with them, so in the winter all you could see was bare earth with the hard-pruned stems of the roses sticking up out of it. I added some pinks, violas, low grey artemisia and I rather forget what else (it was sixty years ago!). I think there may have been some sun roses (*Helianthemum*), possibly the pink-flowered, grey-leaved ones.

There was a not very pretty centrepiece to the garden: a terracotta chimney pot with a small terracotta child kneeling and holding a hollow dish as though to catch the sun. I can imagine Lady Gwendolen in her building operations finding the chimney pot and, with her practical bent, thinking what a good centrepiece it would make as a support for this twee little piece. I wanted very much to remove it and make a small

octagonal pool, with the edge not raised but laid flat in the brickwork, and the octagon outlined in bricks, end to end; and I visualized a fine single jet of water rising from the surface of the pond. However, there was no possibility of turning that small dream into reality. It was only realized years later when one of my sons and his wife, who now live in the lodge, both keen and knowledgeable gardeners, created my imagined pool and fountain, and very pretty it looks.

The raised walk seemed rather unfinished and I put in some more yews to make the hedge run the full length of the path, and in an empty grass plot cut large beds in the turf to grow old-fashioned roses, lilies and other bulbs, planting box to surround the beds.

The soul of the place seemed to lie in the trees, chiefly ancient oaks, some hollow, but still carrying a head of leaves, their life coming from the bark. From acorn to now, they would have watched the birth and death of twenty men, given the average lifespan of an Elizabethan man. Elizabeth I could have ridden by them on her way to and from the great oak she was sitting under when a posse of horsemen rode down to Hatfield from London and knelt at her feet and told her the news that her sister was dead and that she was queen; and too when she rode out to hunt in the park. Some of the oaks are stag-headed, others mere cryptogams, their deep-fissured bark thick with lichens and moss and at their feet the occasional small fern. They all have low canopies of leaves; you will not find a tall-headed ancient oak, for they were pollarded to make the timber for the great ships of the navy, or beams and panelling for houses and palaces. Walnuts are there too, as old as some of the oaks. It was hard to beat the squirrels to the nuts.

But to go back to the oaks for a moment. One of them, not far from the lodge, has a vast circumference. It is quite hollow and now filled

Looking south-west over the walled garden, with its neatly clipped box-edged beds

with cement; its canopy is every year heavy with leaves, and in some years acorns as well. It is named the Lion Oak – why we do not know – and each generation of the family passes on the story that it is mentioned in the Domesday Book.

Writing about the oak trees that surrounded the Lodge House has reminded me of one of my strongest memories of my time there. South of the house was one of these ancient trees, set in a wilderness of tangled grass and brambles, which was the haunt of nightingales. On a warm night in May, with casements open, you listened to their rhapsody of song and could not sleep. It was an insomnia that you would not complain of.

I am aware that I have wandered far from the real subject I set out to write about, the part I played in designing the garden at the Lodge House, but I hope I have wandered to a purpose because what I have written is past history, and the events and the personalities that peopled this past had no small influence on the character of the work I did there.

I tried to think what Lady Gwendolen would have done if she had wanted to expand the garden a little, outside its walls, and hoped that she would have approved of what I did. I took in a piece of land south of the Lodge as far as the great oak where the nightingales sang, to make a croquet lawn. On the east I made a large bed and a narrow border, removing some crazy paving – not a great favourite of mine. A witch hazel (*Hamamelis* × *intermedia* 'Pallida') went in the central bed, a glorious pale lemon-flowered, highly scented plant which flowered very early in the spring; lily of the valley (*Convallaria majalis*), scillas and other spring bulbs went into the border and around the witch hazel.

At the back of this little piece of the garden was an oddly shaped wall. It was the high back of the boiler shed with a most hideously shaped chimney stack, fortunately no longer needed. We pulled the stack down and tried to make an arbour there, but our pockets were rather empty then, and labour almost non-existent, so the arbour did not get far. I think I planted some climbers and left it at that. Near it was a low wooden gate, which led to a patch of rough grassed land with one or two fine trees, many snowdrops in February and a few daffodils later but little else. It was completely shapeless and very untidy. I planted a pair of small *Malus baccata* 'Lady Northcliffe' either side of the gate within this wild patch. She has pretty deep rose-pink buds and white flowers. I planted them in the late forties as quite little trees; they and I have grown old together and now they tower above me, topping me by at least twenty feet.

It was while we were here in the lodge that I resolved always to garden organically. I had never felt easy about herbicides and pesticides and artificial fertilizers. For one thing, they smelt so awful. I knew nothing about what they contained, but 'unwholesome' was a word I attached to them. The awful appearance of plant victims of the herbicide Verdone, which bloated, contorted and chlorosed 'weeds', was painful as well as repellent to see. My love of wild flowers quite got in the way of any practical consideration of labour saving or the beauty of our lawn. I would rather tolerate the weeds as plants in the wrong place; anyway, I liked the clover and the daisies. Besides, how could you safely play with your babies – not to speak of making them daisy chains – on a lawn saturated with herbicide, if it did those awful things to plants? Birds and beneficent insects, lacewings, hoverflies, ladybirds, butterflies and moths were all also being killed. So in 1948 I banned all three products from the garden and later I joined Lawrence Hills' outfit, then called the Henry Doubleday Research Association – after an experimental horticulturist Hills greatly admired, a Quaker who lived in the Victorian era – later HDRA, and now Garden Organic, and felt happier and safer. My friends all thought I was mad, but in the 1960s

Rachel Carson's book *Silent Spring* set off a backlash against pesticides and herbicides,and there was a surge of support for organic gardening. Now almost every one of the herbicides and pesticides called safe in 1948 has been banned by the EU as dangerous to man.

The fountain garden

Good old farmyard manure, calcified seaweed, fish, blood and bone, comfrey and compost – 'muck and magic', as sceptics called them – took the place of artificial fertilizer. When there were no longer any chemicals in the garden birds were encouraged, and all the beneficent insects too, and acid soap for spraying against aphids was a great help – no nematodes were invented then. It takes three years of gardening organically in this way before you can see any change, but then the plants seem to become stronger and more resistant to disease, and there are more beneficent insects about.

When we left the Lodge House, was the garden in better shape than on our arrival six years before? I hope it was, and if it was, it can only have been the result of Lady Gwendolen's creation of the original design; her genius was my inspiration. My son and his wife have added to its beauty with their knowledge, taste and love of plants. It is a joy to return and I feel sure it would be too for Great-aunt T.T.

THE MANOR HOUSE

CRANBORNE, DORSET

The Marquess and Marchioness of Salisbury

It would be hard to imagine that anyone, even someone blind to beauty, could fail to have their eye awoken by their first sight of Cranborne. It is first viewed, wrote David Cecil (my husband's uncle, professor of English literature at Oxford and author of many books), as 'a muddle of stone tiled roofs, set, as manor houses typically are, on the edge of a little town, in the gentle valley of the river Crane which rises in the downland viewed from the Jacobean mount in its garden'.

I shall always remember my first sight of it. We had driven, my parents and I, and my elder sister, from our home in west Dorset near the banks of the River Frome to lunch with the family who lived there.

The road was pretty direct, first through Dorchester, down its main street, past Judge Jeffreys' lodgings, where he dossed for the 'Bloody Assizes', at which he famously sentenced to death followers of the Duke of Monmouth after the 1685 Rebellion; past the grocer's, where my father found his Blue Vinny cheese, made, on Dorset farms where heavy horses were still used, by drawing mouldy harnesses through warm milk (today's Health and Safety officers would faint); past the huge old barn-like building where my mother found treasures of antique furniture from the dear old boy who sold them for a pittance – my mother was very pretty and winning. Then on to Blandford, with its elegant Georgian and Queen Anne houses in rosy brick and Portland stone. There was hardly another car to be met on the road. Ours was a unique one, very slow and old, with a canvas roof and talque windows that let in air all around; thank God, today it was warm, for it was summer. Tabitha, we called the car, and she was capricious. Our ears were attuned to certain noises which heralded the imminent arrest of her engine. Hearts would sink. We knew the consequences of Tabitha's decision to take a breather. Out we would tumble, and this was where my father's years of training in the Royal Navy came to the fore as he commanded his blue jackets, that is us, to get Tabitha going again. With puny force, we pushed and heaved at her fat and convex backside, usually to no avail. As with bicycle riding in the country, we always seemed to be doing this against the wind and uphill. Our greatest dread was that our papa would have to get out the starting handle to crank Tabitha's reluctant engine into life. We had been told that the handle could suddenly crank backwards, and given graphic accounts of this happening, a broken shoulder being the result.

This day was to be a lucky one. Tabitha was in good form and bowled slowly along. I liked her pace, if no one else did. It gave me time to identify the wild flowers along the way. My Bentham and Holker always accompanied me on any expedition. Sanfoin (*Onobryehis viciifolia*) was one of the flowers I remember particularly. It was the first time I had seen it and I remember its beauty as it grew in the field above the road. Now we had arrived at Handley crossroads, where Tess of the d'Urbervilles had

My father at the wheel of
Tabitha, with Ursula, Pamela
and me

walked when she met Angel Clare; this was Hardy country and Cranborne was Chaseborough in Hardy's novel. A couple of miles down the road to the right heading west was the spot where, for a fleeting moment, could be glimpsed the 'muddle of grey tiled roofs'.

Though a little misty and shadowed, that first view still remains with me. Years later, when Cranborne became my home, the picture came into focus, but its sharpness did not change the original vision, and the house and garden for me was always a place of mystery and enchantment.

I was fourteen when I first saw it, dressed in my best summer frock, as was my sister, a prim navy blue with white collar and cuffs. You wore what your mother chose in those days, waiting until you were seventeen before you had a say, although my mama was quite indulgent. There was a friend of hers who gave me a pair of high-heeled shoes, beige canvas with coral-coloured embroidery. I considered them to be the equivalent of today's 'cool' and wobbled about in them for a whole afternoon at the local fête, but the suffering was too much and comfort soon triumphed over vanity.

At that luncheon at Cranborne, I sat next to my future husband, who was the eldest son of the family. We got on very well, though he must have been bored by a fourteen-year-old's conversation. Nevertheless, we played a game of croquet together after lunch.

The next time I was at Cranborne, the game being played was hockey. The war was in its third year and General Alexander was commanding some of the invasion forces just over the hill from Cranborne as head of Southern Command. He was in the enemy hockey team. There was only one rule in the family hockey game, and that was never to lift your stick above your opponent's knee. I took a powerful swipe and caught the General (later Field Marshal) full on the kneecap, which took him out of the game. Of course, no one knew anything about the imminent invasion. It was only after it had happened that the enormity of how the blow on the General's kneecap might have affected the course of the war struck me.

Ten years later, now married to my croquet partner, I came to Cranborne to live. For my husband it was a return, for it had been his home as a child, after his grandfather gave it to his father in 1928. The property had come into my husband's family early in the seventeenth century when the King, James I, had given it to his ancestor, Robert Cecil, 1st Earl of Salisbury and the King's Chief Minister. Up till then, it had been royal property and used by the sovereigns from the time of King John. Legend says that Queen Elizabeth I visited the house in one of her progresses and the saddle in the entrance hall is said to have been hers, while it is recorded in the Cecil papers that during the Civil War the Royalist commander Prince Maurice, brother of Prince Rupert of the Rhine, slaughtered thirty-six sheep in the hall at Cranborne to feed his troops. Charles I visited Cranborne, with his son Henry, that golden boy so full of promise, who died too young, possibly from a dose of poison. There is a bedroom called after the young prince, which is said to have been used by him. We discovered, when redecorating the room, an aumbry, where the vessels for Holy Communion were placed; this was, no doubt, part of a family chapel.

The manor had been one of King John's hunting lodges for the King's use when he took his hounds into the nearby forests of Cranborne Chase. Robert Cecil embellished the simple battlemented building he had been given by considerably enlarging the windows, adding towers to the east and the west on the south front, as well as elaborate Italianate porches to the north and to the south. These last had very probably been designed by Inigo Jones, who was then working at Wilton, Lord Pembroke's house near Salisbury, Wiltshire, and there is a record of a Captain Ryder, Inigo Jones's chief assistant, riding over the downs from Wilton to Cranborne to supervise the building there. He may well, too, have had a hand in the designing of the wing added later to the west of the house. Robert did not neglect the interiors either. To read the contemporary inventories is to have a vision of it as a small Renaissance palace, hung with silks and velvets, tapestries and gilded leather. One upper chamber's decorations were in 'watchet and silver' – that is, sky blue and silver, the Salisbury family colours – and the chamber was filled with pictures and furniture of the finest quality.

The earliest plans of the gardens are those made by John Tradescant, who was gardener to the King and also to Robert Cecil, who employed him to plant his garden at Hatfield in Hertfordshire, a property he had also been given by the King (which I write about on page 54)

Robert gave Tradescant the job of planning and planting the gardens at Cranborne as well, and we know from contemporary papers in the archives at Hatfield that Tradescant visited Cranborne, ordering many plants and taking them down there with him. We have his 'bill of charges' on being sent to plant trees there, and we have his plans for the gardens, though whether they were actually carried out is not known.

There are parts of the garden that date from Tradescant's time and were almost certainly part of his plans. One of them is the double-hedged yew walk, anciently called the Bowling Allée, another the great yew hedge at the back of the Mount Garden and the Mount itself. The stone- and

The south front of the Manor

brick-walled court gardens to the north and south of the manor are also early seventeenth century. The house, however, or a large part of it, is far earlier, going back to the thirteenth and fifteenth centuries. So even the oldest parts of the garden are much younger than the house.

In October 1609, Tradescant's assistant, Mounten Jennings, visited Cranborne, 'being sent thither by your honour's appointment, to survey the garden plot there'. The bill to defray his charges was £5. In December of the same year he was paid £3 14s. 6d. 'for trees brought to Cranborne'. In 1639 there are entries for the cutting of hedges and arbours and the mowing of courts and gardens, as well as 'the planting of XXXVIII ashes in the walk before the house and the mending of Arbors in ye gardens'. Robert Cecil had died in 1612 and been succeeded by his son William, who continued to employ Tradescant. I have mentioned something of the history of the house and garden and Tradescant's connection with it because they had the greatest influence on my ideas and plantings at Cranborne.

I confess to having felt a certain apprehension at the thought of gardening at Cranborne. I had cut my teeth on a small and intimate garden, almost a cottage garden (see the previous chapter), and though

The view from the North Terrace across the North Court and the River Crane to the Avenue. The original trees, Cornish elms (*Ulmus cornubiensis*) were lost to elm disease. The Avenue has been replanted with limes.

Looking down the Beech Avenue
to the twin gatehouses and the
archway that leads to the
southern entrance to the Manor

it was much the same date as Cranborne, the garden here was ten acres larger. Gertrude Jekyll said a garden should 'fit the master and his tastes, just as his clothes do. It should be neither too large or too small but just comfortable.' I felt this master was going to be too small for his clothes. Besides, was the garden not already pretty well perfect? My mother- and father-in-law were knowledgeable and skilled gardeners, and in their years there had added many new beauties to the place. Would there be anything left to do in the way of creating, planning and developing, which are some of the chief pleasures of gardening?

All these poor thoughts soon vanished, as we were overwhelmed by the practical work we immediately had to do if we were to keep the garden – which also included a vegetable garden – going. The labour force had to be halved, leaving four gardeners and a part-timer. We had to decide whether we should put a large area down to grass and try to simplify some of the more elaborate parts of the layout, or sacrifice all the bedding out while reducing the numbers of herbaceous plants. Thank goodness we decided to see if the second plan would do the trick. Economies are always disagreeable. (I remember my husband's brother writing to me from Oxford, where he was studying economics at Christ Church, that he wasn't 'sure he understood them, except that they were something to do with economy of which he didn't approve'.) If we had tried the first plan, some of the yew and box hedges might have gone. However, thanks largely to the hard work, skill and expertise of the splendid team of gardeners we had then, who were with us to the end of our time at the manor, our trimming of the workload succeeded.

Just as the history of the place and Tradescant's work there influenced my ideas for the planning and planting at Cranborne, so too did research and reading on the subject of Tudor and Stuart gardens and gardening, which I now got down to. Hours of enjoyment followed, and happy hours too in gardens where plants grown at that time could be seen.

Gardens of the period were architectural. They were very much extensions of the houses they surrounded and followed strict rules of form, though that did not, I feel sure, prevent even the grandest garden from having an air of simplicity and homeliness about it. This was very true of Cranborne. The walls of the gardens running down from the house form the North and South Courts; the Bowling Allée of clipped yew and the hedges of the Mount Garden, with the grass banks, shaped the green court on the west. The skeleton of Tradescant's garden was there still; he formed these banks to create flat areas for his knots, the great yew hedge at the back of the Mount and the Mount itself, which is charmingly described in an Elizabethan archive as being 'a little hill made to be clambered up to view a fair prospect'. Standing on the top of the Mount you can still see a fair prospect as you look across the valley of the River Crane to the downland beyond.

Now came the time to get down to some serious work in the garden. The soil: that was the first thing to tackle. It could scarcely have been worse, poor, thin and chalky over, in many places, solid chalk. It was quick draining, too, and easily dried out.

A visit from Sir Frederick Stern, the creator of the famous chalk pit garden at Highdown in Sussex and author of *A Chalk Garden*, was helpful. He told me that it was not so much the chalk the plants minded as the fact that they could not get their roots into it. 'Break it up', he said, 'three feet down and round, and it is important not to put the fertilizers and manure too deep. It is best to keep the roots nearer the surface, where they will get more nourishment and can be fed from above. Drought, of course, will be a problem, and a thick mulch in the spring is a help.'

The Mount Garden, an oasis of green with its clipped yew hedges, box edging and swathes of grass

My mother-in-law had built up a remarkable collection of old-fashioned and species roses but now it was painful to look at the poor things. Some were near death and some were already dead. Labels had disappeared. The alkaline soil, lack of feeding, dryness and the war years, when there was very little labour and the call to grow vegetables, had nearly finished them off, and a big rescue operation had to be launched. It would be a very sad thing if the collection were to be lost.

The first thing I did was to take cuttings of all the roses. Many were riddled with that nasty disease blackspot and badly chlorosed. A great deal of manure, leaf mould and compost from the heaps that had been introduced was ladled on to the beds, as well as Maxicrop and fish, blood and bone fertilizer at the appropriate moments. Rather as the human body best resists disease if it is healthy and not junk fed, so must the soil teem with life if plants are to flourish. I banned all chemical fertilizers, sprays and

herbicides, and the garden became an organic one. I was concerned by the smell of these deadly chemicals hanging in the air after the spraying had been done (at least four times a year, starting in January). A smell of death, and so it was.

One year we found on a not too distant farm some exquisite yellow loam. It had a dramatic effect when spread on beds and borders around the poor starved plants, and *Magnolia* × *highdownensis*, which had never grown, shot up like Jack's beanstalk and flowered for the first time.

The old-fashioned flowers and plants with their scents, quiet colours and restful charm – qualities not found often in modern cultivars with greater size and lurid colour – have always had a great appeal to me. With Tradescant's lists and my mind full of pictures of Tudor and Stuart gardens, I planted his 'great white roses', the Albas, in the North Court, which was to be a white garden, with a scattering of pale buffs and apricots, which seem to emphasize the whiteness of the other flowers.

I planted more roses to build up and replace those lost from my mother-in-law's collection, mostly Damasks, Gallicas and Centifolias, along with some Hybrid Musks and species roses. These last flourished in the miserable chalk soil, which was endearing of them, and threw up great arching branches, fifteen to twenty feet high. *Rosa forrestiana* was a beauty, and so were R. × *hibernica*, R. 'Cantabrigensis', and R. *moyesii* with its wine-dark flowers. I planted herbs in the beds and borders, thyme, hyssop and savory, along with pinks, violas and cistus, daphnes and lavenders, these taking the place of bedding and herbaceous plants, and they were underplanted with spring, summer and autumn bulbs.

Above One of the old-fashioned roses
Opposite The west entrance to the North Court

Under the crab apples in the orchard, I planted quantities of autumn crocus, reviving memories of meadows in France, where the pale goblets of 'the little naked boys' grow in the close-scythed grass.

The beds and borders were thickly planted to clothe the ground, using such grey plants as artemisias, lavender and helichrysum, as well as the evergreen of daphnes, the blue-grey of 'Jackman's Blue' rue and the spiked leaves of *Iris germanica* to help them still look furnished in the winter. This thick planting, with the addition of a heavy mulch, helped to keep the weeds down.

The kitchen garden was very large, surrounded and divided in two by twelve-foot-high chalk walls; cob walls they were called, and today the art of making them is lost. They were built up layer by layer in wooden screens, the chalk mixed with grit and chopped heath or heather. Against the southern side and east end of this chalk wall I made a Sweet Garden, which is largely a herb garden. You entered through an archway in a yew hedge – as high as the wall – which surrounded it. I cut 'portholes' in the southern wall of the hedge so that you could look out to the meadow and trees beyond, which bordered the grounds and screened the road.

I planted a long narrow bed, divided by a seat and backed by a hedge of sweet briar, with lily of the valley. These plants, if they are to flower well, are very greedy feeders and the bed had a dose of manure every year. The eight beds for the herbs and sweet-scented flowers and leaves were hedged with lavender cotton (*Santolina chamaecyparissus*). In the centre there was a stone sundial, which was said to be part of a pillar that came from the priory that existed here before Henry VIII's dissolution of the monasteries. (I like the lines Hilaire Belloc, on a visit to the house, wrote of this sundial: 'I am a sundial and I make a botch/Of what is done far better by a watch.')

The banks of the monks' stew ponds above the River Crane are still visible below the main bridge in the garden over the river. Four standards of Early Dutch honeysuckle (*Lonicera belgica*) were planted in the four beds nearest to this sundial. A seat, looking south, divided the wall, with climbing roses and jasmine above it.

One of the main roses is *R. cerascarpa*, now, I think, out of commerce. It has huge trusses of white, very scented flowers. A friend, admiring, thought I had told him its name was 'Sarah Scarper' and spent much time searching for it in rose lists. I took cuttings and it now grows at both Hatfield and Saint Clou, the château in Provence which I write about on page 106.

This was a delicious garden to work in, as the varied scents clung to one's clothes throughout the day.

Coming back through the yew archway, you found yourself in a long broad walk with a border under the high chalk wall. This border was a narrow one when I came, in spite of a planting of all shrubs and trees, including two very large Judas trees (*Cercis siliquastrum*), the *Magnolia × highdownensis*, some viburnums and species roses. The high wall seemed to need a wider border, so I increased its width by three feet, filling the newly created spaces with more favourite shrubs, large and small, and some more species roses. I cut windows in the high yew hedge opposite and planted more of a crab apple, *Malus* 'Hillieri', that was already growing there in a straight line down from the original. This malus has arching stems wreathed in crimson-budded semi-double flowers of bright pink. It was a fine sight in late spring.

Leaving this walk through another archway cut in a high yew hedge, you came into a garden I

The view from the Mount Garden of the west front of the house , possibly designed by Inigo Jones, with the south and north porches

designed quite late in my time at Cranborne. It is a simple knot with an octagon pool in its centre, outlined in brick; the beds are hedged in box and planted with a collection of thymes. A beech hedge surrounds it on three sides, with an Italian seventeenth-century stone seat on the south, and in a niche cut in the beech on the west an Italian stone statue of a hunter, complete with a bird in his hand and a dog by his side, and wearing a rather fetching tricorn hat.

A great deal of planting was done in the garden over the years we were there, some quite early in our time, some later or much later. I planted oaks, tolerant of alkaline soil, in the wooded area above the southern entrance to the house; white pinks in quantity, in the borders backed by ancient espaliered apples, with trunks and branches like fossils, in the North Court garden's central walk; and above the River Crane a large rectangle of wild grass, with a collection of various large-fruited crab apples underplanted with pale-flowered narcissus.

One of the major changes we made was along the length of the river that flowed through the garden. It was a winter bourn, which rose in the autumn and dried up in the summer. There was talk of sinking a borehole so that there would be water throughout the year, but somehow the talk never turned into action. It was very tempting to garden there, as the soil was reasonably acid. We had a large quantity of stone from a demolished manor house in the Isle of Purbeck, which was, like Cranborne's, from a quarry at Chilmark, now worked out. We used this to line the sides of the river and to form two square ponds either side of the bridge leading from the North Court into an avenue of Cornish elms beyond.

There were already some species roses planted by my mother-in-law on the southern side of the river and a narrow border in front of a tapestry hedge which screened this part of the garden from the field beyond. Now between the path and the river I made beds that ran the length of it within the garden, and

The simple knot garden I designed for Cranborne towards the end of my time there. The box-edged, thyme-filled beds are surrounded by tall beech hedges.

The Knot Garden, with the statue of St Fiacre overlooking the box-edged beds filled with flowers grown in Tradescant's time

Bailey, the estate's skilled stonemason, built a charming little stone and cobbled bridge to cross the water at the far end. I piled leaf mould and peat on the new beds and felt triumphant when blue poppies (*Meconopsis*) flourished there.

A new addition to the garden was a knot, which I designed for a blank piece of lawn to the south of the west wing and behind the west wall of the South Court. Here I was harking back to Tradescant's plans for the garden, for he certainly had knotted beds around the house. In the box-edged beds, I used only those plants grown in the sixteenth and seventeenth centuries and especially those known to have been planted at Cranborne by Tradescant. Generous friends gave me early pinks, the rose plantain, double sweet rocket, Gerard's double primroses, auriculas, the double and the single, and the plumed hyacinth, as well as the stately crown imperial without which no knot garden was complete in the seventeenth century.

Facing the garden, with his back to a niche in a tall box hedge, was a statue we had found in Italy of St Fiacre, the patron saint of gardeners. St Fiacre went as a pilgrim to Compostela and the statue is dressed in the garb of Sir Walter Raleigh's 'Passionate Pilgrim':

> Give me my scallop-shell of quiet,
> My staff of faith to walk upon,
> My scrip of joy, immortal diet,
> My bottle of salvation,
> My gown of glory, hope's true gage,
> And thus I'll take my pilgrimage.

His face is holy, and as you look at it, Robert de Condamines' words come to mind: 'The saint has come into the garden . . . From his little cell he has come out into the evening air to look upon the roses. One walks with him and the ministry of angels is with him.'

We had John Tradescant's plan for the South Court. This had been altered in the nineteenth century into a circle of grass with a gravel drive around it. While incorporating its paved paths, I wanted too to put his knots into each corner, but these never got done. It was 'One day I will do it . . .'! So, slightly modifying Tradescant's plan, we paved and cobbled the court, introducing a very simple Italian stone-rimmed fountain in the centre and four large box spheres at each corner, with a pair of Italian stone Renaissance greyhounds sitting either side of the South Porch and large Italian stone vases planted with cypresses. These last had a romantic history. They were grown from seeds my son picked from cypress trees growing in Sicily, near the Roman temple at Agrogento, during a March visit to the island and brought home in his pocket. The court has once again been changed, and these cypress trees have been taken to France and are now growing by the river in the garden of Saint Clou.

It would be difficult, I think, for anyone not to regret leaving Cranborne, even if only a day had been spent there, but in my case regret was tempered by several things. One was that I knew well and was very fond of Hatfield, where we were going to live, and another that for a few years we were to live in both places until my son retired from the House of Commons and went with his family to live at the manor. So it was a long-drawn-out sigh of farewell, ending in the joy of the family continuing to live there as they had done for over three hundred years.

A GARDEN IN THE WEST COUNTRY

I have a cousin in the West Country and, as the French say, *'on s'entend bien'*. Although there was nearly half a generation's difference in our ages, we found much to be enjoyed in our cousinly relationship and in each other's company. This was especially so during the early years of my marriage. I had six boys and one girl, she five girls and one boy; our younger boys and her son were well matched in age and friends with one another. We both liked hunting and sometimes joined up to have a day with the local hounds. But not all her interests were as mine, nor all mine as hers: notably, she had a passion for archaeology and I had a lack of interest in it, and I had a love of gardening and she had a dislike of it. When we visited each other and talked together about our respective gardens, and I was indulging in some gardening enthusiasm, she would say, 'I'm not in the least interested in plants or gardens.'

After the passing of a few years, I was surprised when one day my cousin told me that she had decided to do up her walled garden, and please would I design it for her. When I had recovered from my astonishment and pondered the invitation, the offer became an alluring and rather enjoyable prospect.

What would it involve, I wondered? I had only designed the gardens of the houses I lived in, so this would be a very different proposition from every point of view. Her garden was a large one, three and a half acres, and enclosed by brick walls. It had belonged to a house built in 1742 on the same site of a seventeenth-century building that had been demolished.

In 1971, the year I received the invitation, the garden, as I remember it, was virtually derelict, the enclosure a blank canvas for me to draw on, to plan, design and plant. My cousin, despite her lack of interest in flowers and plants, liked the thought of reviving this dead and neglected place where once there had been a working and thriving kitchen garden with greenhouses, now empty and forlorn but no doubt once growing white Muscat grapes and peaches and tender plants to decorate the house.

It is more than thirty-five years since I worked on this place, so I may well have forgotten some of the details of the plans I made for it, and especially some of the planting. The land within the walls was flat, with no feature except for a six-foot-wide 'canal', which crossed the garden diagonally and was filled with water. Crossing this canal halfway down its length was a simple flat wooden bridge. A greenhouse, the gardener's cottage, and a brick and stone summerhouse were built against the brick walls; these were twelve feet high in most places, but rose to fourteen feet or more behind the houses. The entrance to the garden was an exceptionally grand and original one: tall brick pillars, stone capped and crowned by stone balls, framed a brick arched gateway closed by an iron gate of rare beauty, wrought with stylized leaves, flowers and bunches of grapes – a fit entrance to a significant space. What I had to do now was to try to fill this space with a significant garden.

The gardener's cottage, looking out over the canal, now filled with water-loving plants and bordered by hedging

I began the work by measuring the space and testing the soil. This last was chalk, with a good two feet of rich friable soil above it, resulting from nearly 250 years of cultivation with well-rotted manure and vegetable matter. I then drew up a plan and a planting scheme. The garden was to be a decorative one, with ample room for flowers as well as fruit and vegetables, and incorporating a herb garden. I had a friend who was an architect, a delightful man, who had done some work for us at Cranborne. He was a gardener as well as an architect, sharing a love I had for sweet geraniums, of which he had a fine collection, and we would exchange cuttings. He kindly drew the plan to scale for me. Then the site was levelled, the design marked out and the planting began.

In the new design there was a broad central path, which led to the main entrance, and in two places along its length were circular spaces with a canopy over them, formed by iron frames. These frames had roses, clematis and white wisteria grown over them. Other narrower paths divided large box-edged beds, which were planted, some with flowers and some with vegetables. A broader path led to the summerhouse, another to a circular herb garden with narrow brick paths outlining its beds and an ancient stone and carved sundial at its centre. This had two circles of stone steps and one final square supporting the dial, so you had to climb a little to see what time the gnomon was marking.

I made two tunnels, the arches in iron, supporting different apple varieties, and these tunnels led into a circle of golden-fruited crab apples. For the making of the ironwork, I enlisted the help of my village blacksmith, who gallantly

Left, above The view to the sundial from the rose-covered canopy
Left, below Looking from a blossoming arbour to the wrought-iron gate, down a walk with apple espaliers and *Helleborus orientalis*
Right The summerhouse from the box parterre

embraced this unusual commission and carried it out to perfection.

I was swiftly warming up to my first commission and with encouragement and cousinly approval launched into further plantings in the now fast-developing garden.

A walk bordered with pear trees appeared and a hedged compartment of apple trees, roses, clematis and other climbers was planted against the walls. A half circle of paving at the foot of the wall with a pair of decorative wooden seats had one of the main paths leading to it. I also created brick-paved areas, about four or five feet wide, from the path to the walls, with broad, flat-topped blocks of box between them.

The flower garden was generously planted with roses, peonies, phlox, lavenders and rosemary as well as cistus and other small shrubs, with the beds bordered by box hedges, I planted more small flowering trees – cherries and crab apples amongst them – in hedged enclosures, along with a walk framed by pleached limes.

These last works completed the garden. Of course, if a garden is yours, it is never finished, and I did at this moment have a passing thought that my cousin, now that she had one of her own, might one day develop a comparable frame of mind.

Surprise, surprise! On subsequent visits, I found her busily weeding in it, so industriously that I was led to protest that I had not come over only to have to address her bottom. But in spite of the limits on conversation, what a pleasure it was to witness her interest and involvement!

Far left, above The sundial with the orchard beyond
Far left, below The grass walks through the box parterre, with a fine *Pyrus salicifolia* to the left
Left Views of the box parterre

BROADLANDS

HAMPSHIRE

Lord and Lady Brabourne

Amongst the first designing jobs I did, apart from the gardens surrounding the houses I had lived in, were the Pleasure Gardens at Broadlands in Hampshire, the home of Lord and Lady Mountbatten and after their deaths the home of Lord Mountbatten's grandson Lord Romsey, now Lord Brabourne.

The land on which Broadlands stands had been owned by Romsey Abbey since before the Norman Conquest, as was the manor house that stood there, but after the dissolution of the monasteries it was sold, in 1547, to Sir Francis Fleming. In 1736, Henry Temple, the 1st Lord Palmerston, bought the house and it was he who began the creation of the formal gardens between the house and the River Test.

The architect Henry Holland transformed the early house, changing its Jacobean façade into a classic Palladian one, and the house you see today is the one created in 1760 when the 2nd Lord Palmerston lived there. It was then that Lancelot 'Capability' Brown came on the scene, and some of his planting in the park survives. Of Brown's work in Hampshire that still survives, Broadlands is probably one of the most complete

Over the years, several designers were commissioned to work on the gardens at Broadlands, one being W.A. Nesfield, who designed the parterre on the south side of the house, but little of the work that he did survives. Lord Palmerston took an interest in the fruit in the walled gardens; Lady Mount Temple, second wife of Wilfred Ashley, Lord Mount Temple (who had inherited Broadlands and was the father of Edwina Mountbatten) gave Constance Spry one of her first commissions, which was to design the White Garden at Broadlands.

My grandmother-in-law spent some of her childhood at Broadlands in the company of her cousin Ettie Fane; both were orphans, and related to the Palmerston family. Ettie later married Lord Desborough, becoming a leading light in that elect coterie the Souls, and mother of the poet Julian Grenfell. I heard from my grandmother-in-law something of her memories of Broadlands during her days spent there as a child, which seem from her account to have been happy ones. Lady Salisbury remained close to Cousin Ettie all her life, and physically close as well, for their houses, after their marriages, were only a few miles apart, and my grandmother-in-law told me they communicated with each other every day.

I paid one visit to Broadlands from Cranborne with my in-laws, early in my marriage. It was a very grand occasion, I remember – Lord Mountbatten, dressed in full uniform, made a long speech, all the ladies wore hats and gloves, and a military band played striking tunes – but I formed no impression of the garden, apart from noting a large round stone-edged fountain and well-mown lawns crowded with people. Lord Mountbatten had not been interested in the gardens, but he took a keen interest in the planting of trees in the Pleasure Grounds by members of royal families and other notable guests, and there are many fine trees that were planted by them to commemorate their visits.

It was early in 1984 that Lady Romsey got in touch with me to ask if I felt I 'could take in hand' the gardens at Broadlands. The Pleasure Grounds had been neglected and were overgrown and in need of much attention; these had now been cleared and were ready to be planned and planted, though, Lady Romsey said, 'A good deal more than energy is now required.'

There was water in the Pleasure Grounds in the shape of a stream, called the Japanese Stream because a Japanese garden had, in the reign of Queen Victoria (a time when such gardens were very fashionable), been made near by, its water coming from the River Test. Places along this stream and some other large, rather bare areas were now crying out for some landscaping and new planting.

In May 1984, I began work by surveying the area and getting information about the climate and the soil. I submitted a prospectus, which I will quote from here, as it gives an idea of my thoughts and suggestions for the landscaping and planting of the Pleasure Grounds.

'The site is a most attractive one with the river to the south and the Japanese Stream forming with the steep bank to the north a delightful "enclosure". The area has some interesting mature plantings formed by some fine trees, but it does have some considerable disadvantages, which will limit to an extent the choice of trees, plants and bulbs for the site. However, these disadvantages could I think, be mitigated considerably if certain things are done, and I will make some proposals later on.

'The area is damp and in some places a wet one open to a fierce west wind, but I think a great deal of its charm lies in being able to look over areas of grass to the river with the play of light and shade and being able to look through the trees and down clearings in them to the Japanese Stream and the bank beyond.

'Therefore, I feel that the area would be best kept open. This is not to say that a considerable number of young specimen trees should not be introduced. A large number on the site are already very mature and plantings that will eventually replace them should certainly be considered and also to help combat the wind problem.

'Nonetheless, I do not think it is an area which would be improved by heavy planting; in fact from the aesthetic point of view, I feel it is an area which should be rather lightly planted.

'A great deal could be done with the planting of spring, early summer, summer and autumn bulbs, corms and tubers. Also with the planting of perennial, biennial and some annual wild flowers, not only in the grass but also along the bank above the Japanese Stream.

'I feel that a number of hardwoods should be planted such as oak, beech, ash and lime in variety and some other trees, chiefly deciduous, well suited to the soil and site. Further planting of some smaller ornamental trees such as acer (not *Acer japonica*), sorbus and betula could be made with advantage.

'I feel that all ornamental trees verging on the sophisticated – what might be termed "garden" trees, such as Japanese cherries, hybrid malus, laburnum and hybrid prunus, should be avoided – species trees, plants and bulbs seem to be more suitable for the "wildness" of the site and I think would be more in harmony with their surroundings. I am not suggesting a rigid purity in this but do feel that the plantings, to be in character, should look like "wild creatures" not garden hybrids.

'If the wild flowers are to succeed on this site, the grass must be cut after the seed is ripe and ready to fall. This would be at the earliest, during the last days of July and preferably in the first week in August. For instance, ophrys [wild orchis] seed and that of martagon lilies is seldom ripe before then. Ideally the last cut should be in November and the first as early in the year as is practical. Occasionally some early bulbs would have to be cut around.

'I would advise some drainage of parts of the site, probably with land drains, as it is a damp one with two wet areas one of which is very wet, otherwise I think the mowing at the current time would be a problem.

'A hedge should be introduced to mask the wire fence protecting the Pleasure Grounds from the public. Also the line could be improved at the lower river end of the fence, but this could be done without moving the fence. The hedge would take a different line here. I suggest the hedge should not be a high one but just high enough to screen the wire, and that it should be a "tapestry" hedge of yew, holly, box and an occasional beech plant, both green and copper.

'This would look less formal – less "garden-y", but I feel that if the approach to the Pleasure Grounds is going to be a visual pleasure, the wire fence should be as invisible as possible.

'I would suggest that there should be "walks" through the area, ideally of mown grass wide enough for two people to walk comfortably side by side. One walk would go along the Japanese Stream, and a little out from it, the other along the river much as it does now. One or two other mown paths could link the two walks at certain points, but the main perambulation would be a "round" as if it were taking the perambulators along stream and river and able to regard vistas and clearings, as they move along the paths.

'The planting would be carried out to fit in with these walks, to be visually attractive when viewed from them and satisfying to the eye as the walker passes along them. The present beds with small azaleas, which are not suited to the soil or the site, should be removed as well as the beds of spirea and the smaller malus and possibly the crataegus. These could perhaps be used elsewhere in the gardens.

'I suggest that the sundial would be better removed, as it seems to be out of place and scale here. Could this be put elsewhere in the garden in a formal setting? I feel that all formality should be eliminated from the site as being unsuitable to this particular area.

'There are one or two trees I would suggest could be removed with advantage, notably the *Prunus pissardii* and the two salix. Also could the walnuts that are not thriving be moved, in spite of the fact that they were planted many years ago, to the place where the other walnuts are thriving at the eastern end of the Pleasure Grounds? Of course, there is always a risk that they might not survive but if suitably prepared and swiftly carried out at the right season, I think the move could give them a good chance of survival.

'Along the bank above the Japanese Stream there could be a certain amount of clearing done and planting or with small ornamental and flowering trees, these being under planted with things such as vines, ferns, wild honeysuckle, *Daphne pontica*, snowdrops, *Narcissus pseudonarcissus*, bluebells, species crocus, autumn crocus, colchicum, *Lamium galeobdolon*. This bank could be a most attractive feature but its great usefulness could be in providing a protective screen to the site from the north, and with this end in view I should advise planting along the top of the bank a good screen of trees. I would also advise that the southwest end of the area of the Pleasure Ground to be more thickly planted to try and cut the force of the west wind a little.

'There is a path from the Pleasure Grounds up the bank, which seems to curve for no particular reason. I think it would be much more pleasing if it were straight.

'I have doubts about the *Robinia pseudoacacia* 'Frisia's being quite suitable here. They are a beautiful tree but perhaps a little out of place. However, if it should be decided to keep them, I suggest a small grove of them should be planted – at least several more.

'If it is possible to do some drainage of the site, it would certainly help to establish the wild flowers and bulbs more satisfactorily as the grass could be mown more frequently and at the right times as I have already mentioned above. If this is done, I would suggest sowing ox-eye daisies, cowslips (these are best grown in a row or rows in the kitchen garden and the seed collected each year and grown on, the young plants being put out in the areas to colonise).

'Primroses should be established in the same way especially on the bank along the Japanese Stream. Forget-me-not seed could be scattered in open areas where the grass is less thick, also *Aquilegia* of the old-fashioned "granny's bonnet" type, these could be established along the bank. Martagon lilies, and in the dry places some species tulips, could be grown such as *Tulipa didieri*, *grengiolensis*, *sylvestris* and *marjolleti*, all indigenous species in Europe and *sylvestris* is a British wild flower. *Ornithogalum nutans* and *umbellatum* should colonize in the grass as well as Martagon lilies for summer flowering, *Crocus sativus* and *speciosus* as well as some *Colchicum autumnale* for autumn flowering should do well.

'In the damp areas, meadow sweet (*Filipendula*) and *Cardamine pratensis* (lady's smock) as well as marsh marigolds could be established along with other damp lovers. If it were decided not to do any drainage of the area, I think it would have to be accepted that the grass could not be cut sufficiently often to keep it reasonably short (that is it would not be able to have a November or March cut except in very exceptional years) and then the plantings in the grass would have to be tempered to its condition.

'I would suggest that an expert in drainage should be consulted (perhaps you have one on the estate), to see if the wetness in the area could be somewhat reduced. This seems to me to be the key to decisions to be made on the type of planting to be done and to what is to be the final aspect of the Pleasure Grounds.'

To a degree, I have to rely on my memories, as 1984 is quite a long way back in my life – all of twenty-three years – though I am helped by scale plans, as well as lists of trees, plants and wild flower seeds. These last were for planting in the grass in the open areas. Oxslips, cowslips and primroses were to go in the places they would be happiest in, some out in the open sunny areas, and others under the trees, while autumn and spring cyclamen would go under trees in half shade. I have found a considerable list of bulbs that I suggested should be planted – spring and autumn crocus, ornithogalums, small narcissus and the native wild daffodil, *Narcissus pseudonarcissus* (Wordsworth's daffodil), as well as *Vinca major* and *V. minor* – and these bulbs have, Lady Brabourne says, done well. Perhaps rather too optimistically I advised – I see from another list – the purchase of bulb seed from a nursery in Holland. These included *Tulipa* and *Scilla* species, chionodoxa and erythroniums.

Lady Romsey accepted my proposals and the first phase of the planting commenced in 1984. I remember noting that the banks of the stream were rather denuded of trees, and I selected several especially ornamental ones that should flourish there, delighting in getting roots near water and into damp places. *Pteracarya fraxinifolia* was one, and others were *Prunus avium* and its double version, as well as another relation, *Prunus padus* 'Watereri'. There were already one or two alders on the banks of the stream, and they are such decorative quick-growing trees, having the advantage of being almost evergreen, keeping their leaves well into the new year, that I planted another one, *Alnus rubra*. There was some unattractive laurel by the steam, and this came out, some willows taking its place, but which variety of *Salix* I do not remember; *Metasequoia glyptostroboides*, the dawn redwood, happy in damp places, went by the steam too.

The planting in the Pleasure Grounds was done in two phases, the planting along the stream being phase one. Phase two was planting that was done further afield, where there were dips and rises and slopes here and there. I remember choosing an open sunny spot for that beautiful ash *Fraxinus oxycarpa* 'Raywood', which likes a dry, well-drained soil. And then there was a tulip tree (*Liriodendron tulipifera*), which in maturity produces tulip-like flowers, yellow green outside and orange within. It is perfectly hardy and will grow to a great height. In the New York Botanical Garden in the Bronx, there is a magnificent double allée of these trees, which turn amber and yellow in the autumn and in winter are a glorious sight with a carpet of snow beneath them; one, known as the mother tree, is over a hundred feet tall. A good-sized open space had to be chosen for the tree at Broadlands, not only for the tree to have room to expand but so that it could be viewed and admired in its full beauty. Besides a group of white-stemmed birches and several varieties of oak trees, there were a couple of tall-growing magnolias, and trees that were ornamental in that they bore decorative blossom and fruits such as malus and sorbus, the last with different varieties carrying glorious pink or white or golden fruits.

Broadlands was an interesting design and planting job for me to do, for it was the first I had ever done in which the house was not involved in the design; what made it even more interesting was that the land I designed and planted had first been laid out and planned by Capability Brown. It was therefore a rather intimidating assignment, but in spite of that a very enjoyable one, and as far as experience was concerned, most helpful when later I was asked to do other work which involved designing a landscape.

HATFIELD HOUSE

HERTFORDSHIRE

The Marquess and Marchioness of Salisbury

My first sight of Hatfield was late in the summer of 1945. I had just become engaged to the eldest grandson of the 4th Marquess of Salisbury, the direct descendant of Robert Cecil, who had built the house in the early seventeenth century and became First Minister to King James I. His father, Lord Burghley, had held the same position with Queen Elizabeth I, and Robert was his second son. My fiancé was also called Robert.

I was twenty-three then and had been scarcely grown up when war broke out in September 1939. Educated by governesses, or non-educated, as my adored father believed educating women only taught them how to argue with men, I had studied for a few months at the Royal Drawing School, before being plunged into war work. My first job was looking after pathetic little evacuees, miserable and utterly lost, clutching on to their only link to Mum and Dad and home, a satchel or toy, too stunned to cry and spurning the carefully prepared meat and two veg, wanting only sausages and tinned peas.

Later a desperate cry from a Red Cross commandant friend took me to Sheerness – Shere-nastiness, as it was well named – to cook, clean and make beds for trainee nurses. I had never been away from home before (grandparents' houses didn't count) and I felt horribly homesick. Next came training to become a Red Cross nurse. I had never done a serious exam before, and was amazed to pass two, First Aid and Home Nursing. Walking home one day in my new uniform, which I was to wear for the next four and a half years, I saw a man, apparently *in extremis*, face down in the road. Ah! I thought, though my heart thumped in nervous anticipation, here is a chance to practise my new skills. 'Are you hurt? Can I help?' I said. He turned his face to me. 'Don't worry about me, Miss,' he said. 'I'm only looking for a pipe.'

Next came the years working as a nurse in military hospitals. The most dramatic and heartrending moments were when the wounded men came straight from the battlefields after Dunkirk and the Normandy landings, still in their bloodied uniforms. I loved my charges. They were so patient, so brave and uncomplaining; cheerful and funny too, no matter how badly wounded or impaired.

The ones that came from Lancashire were my especial favourites, though I tried not to show it. When I was on night duty, I sometimes had to tend a dying man. One wanted to be with them all the time, but you might be the only nurse, apart from the night sister, in a ward of thirty-six and it was rarely possible. One felt agonized that they had no mother or father, or at least a family member or a loving friend or pastor with them.

For years after the war, I had letters from my old patients. One, a Scotsman, wrote remarkable letters; Armour he was called, intelligent, educated (unlike his nurse) – a literary man. I found my Scotsmen

The East Parterre, the Maze and the New Pond

notably better educated than the English. Now, in 2007, there are two of my old patients I still correspond with.

You may, my reader, be well justified in asking what all this has to do with the designing of the gardens at Hatfield. I was led astray when my memories were awakened by writing about my first visit there, which was only a brief time after my leaving the military hospital. I must quickly return to *mes moutons*.

In 1945 Hatfield was bleak and war worn. Its once rosy-red brick was blackened by coal-fired trains from the nearby station and the coal smoke from the chimneys of London only nineteen miles away. Gravel surrounded the house, its north front with cold blank plate-glass windows, put in by the 3rd Marquess, three times Prime Minister to Queen Victoria; he was superb at that job, but in these matters quite without taste.

It had a gloomy dejected air, but one's eye had become attuned by the dirt and devastation of London, so one was not as surprised or shocked by it as one would be now. It had been a military hospital throughout the war, and was in as bad a state inside as it was outside, the panelling boarded up, empty of furniture and every floor covered in tasteful mud-brown army linoleum. There was a lingering smell of Dettol and much dust. Even then I remember thinking how isolated the house looked from the garden that should have been around it. This, from glimpses I saw, looked like the house, sad and neglected.

We drove on down to the Lodge House, which I write about on page 18. Robert wanted us to live there and I was immediately enchanted by this delicious house, looking as one would have imagined the house in 'Goldilocks and the Three Bears' to have looked.

However, for nearly two years after we married, I lived in Hatfield House with Robert's grandparents while his considerable war wounds were being dealt with by the incomparable Mr McIndoe, who restored their lives to so many burnt and damaged RAF pilots. It was a happy time for me. I quickly came to love dearly my grandparents-in-law, and to love the house. In spite of its war-worn state, its atmosphere and its owners enfolded one in a welcoming warmth and tranquillity.

I had time to explore the garden and it was during these months spent at Hatfield that ideas of how it might look, should the sea of gravel be swept away to be replaced by surroundings something more in harmony with the great house, began to form in my mind. Many years were to pass before dreams could become reality, for we only came to live at Hatfield in 1972 after my father-in-law had died. It was the start of an idyll, which ended only when I left after Robert's death in 2003, two years before we were to celebrate our diamond wedding.

It was rather daunting to realize that the gardens were now my responsibility to run, and perhaps to redesign and to develop, but it was a challenge too, and, casting all diffidence and uncertainty behind me, I enthusiastically and joyously took it up. It was quite a task but one that made me spoilt for pleasure for over thirty years.

The great house that Robert Cecil built still stands, much as he built it, save for some details. Elizabethan and Stuart gardens, although in many ways homely and simple, were architectural too, and in a subtle way adhered to strict rules of form. They were very much extensions of the house they surrounded, and with it formed a blended whole most comfortable to the eye. This must have been very true of Hatfield: the walls of the courts were close to the house, much closer than they are now. The house when I first saw it was divorced from its gardens, and its surroundings had been much changed, to something that seemed altogether alien to it.

My first thought was to try to replace, as far as possible, the intimacy between the house and its gardens. At the same time I had to accept that without the mind, feelings and outlook of those gardeners of long ago, and with so much irrevocably altered, it would be quite impossible aesthetically or financially to attempt to replicate physically what they had created. However, I learnt all that it was possible to learn about the original garden made by Robert Cecil and his son, as well as something of the work there of John Tradescant, who was head gardener from 1610 until Cecil's death in 1612 and to whom Cecil entrusted the planting of the garden, and Salomon de Caus, one of the foremost garden designers of the day. My ideas, plans and plantings at Hatfield in the last years were profoundly influenced by this knowledge. Starting with Tradescant's lists of plants and trees, the descriptions of the gardens in the seventeenth century and everything I was able to glean from papers and bills in the archives, I went on to read all the literature I could on the gardens and plants of the period and to visit other gardens of this time, in England and abroad, especially those in Italy, a country that had so much influenced Cecil's work at Hatfield. Knowing roughly the plan of the garden at Hatfield in the seventeenth century helped a picture to form gradually in my mind's eye of the gardens as they may have looked in the seventeenth century.

I felt, as the Elizabethans and Stuarts did, that I did not want to break with the past. They, simply, by following their principles of beauty and sense of form, tried to make lovelier all that was most attractive in medieval times. I looked at how Jacobean gardens had developed from the earlier gardens of Classical and Roman times, through those in Renaissance Italy, which had widely influenced the designers in France, from where these new ideas crept slowly over to England.

My greatest problem was to decide where to begin the restoration of the gardens. The canvas was so huge. Mercifully, the problem was decided for me by the absolute priority of restoring the Muniment Room, where precious archives and books were kept. The room had been built in the nineteenth century and was letting in damp, had no environmental controls, and had become quite unfit for its purpose.

It took the best part of three years to restore the Muniment Room. The East Terrace was dug up, the rooms underneath made waterproof and the terrace reinstated. During this process, to our great excitement, we discovered the line of the original Jacobean terrace. Faced by the same bricks as the house, it was, as we had suspected, much narrower and three feet lower than the one built in the nineteenth century. It was enormously tempting to reinstate the original, which would have restored the proper proportions of the house, but this was a dream that could not be fulfilled and a compromise had to be reached. The dreaded gravel which surrounded the whole house was removed from the terrace and grass and paving laid instead, and a low wall in Jacobean-proportioned bricks topped with Portland stone took the place of the Victorian openwork wall on the terrace's eastern edge.

The very ugly nineteenth-century garden staircase had to be taken down to allow work on the Muniment Room, and it was at this point that the Italian influence came into play. The terrace looked down on a series of descending terraces, much as many Italian gardens do. Why not build a perron in stone, of two descending staircases to the right and left with stone balustrading? We had seen similar designs in Italy and returned to look at them and others. Meanwhile, we remembered we had found in Italy, many years earlier, four seventeenth-century stone statues, which had come from a villa near Lake Como. When these were taken out of store they appeared to be entirely sympathetic to the design, and the right size and proportions, with all the figures looking outward as though surveying a distant view.

Opposite The East Parterre and the Maze from the east terrace, overlooked by one of the seventeenth-century Italian statues we placed on the balustrade
Left The East Parterre looking towards the east terrace, with the massive forms of the 'mitred bishop' box topiary in the centre of the beds

But could they be relied on still to look in proportion once placed on the pillars of the balustrade? It seemed unwise to fix them without trying them, but how to pose these high and heavy creatures without the great danger of their toppling over and crashing below? They were too heavy to be held. Even our intrepid stonemasons, never before stumped for an answer, could not think of a way. Then I had an idea. Ask four of the smallest men on the estate to come and pose, drape them in dustsheets and hey presto! There was the answer. The proportions seemed to be good, a photograph was taken and there were smiles, not to say laughs, all round.

Once the terrace had been laid with turf and paving, attention could be given to its planting. There were already several good plants against the walls of the house, including a rose 'Albéric Barbier' and a *Magnolia grandiflora*, which had, in the past, always been severely pruned and had never flowered. I allowed it to grow away from the wall, and this has encouraged it to flower abundantly. A deciduous magnolia, *M. denudata*, the yulan tree, was also there, one of four of this beautiful tree, planted against the walls of the house in the late nineteenth century. I added a *Paulownia fargesii*, whose buds, if they escape frost (as they are formed by September), come into flower in May.

I had read somewhere that a paulownia should always be planted where it can be looked down on. Here was the perfect position to see if this was right and it was. In the weeks of May, from the windows of the State Drawing Room, you can look down on a veritable surging sea of cream and heliotrope-purple scented flowers.

The Italian influence continued with the planting in 1977 of two walks running east and west framed by holm oaks (*Quercus ilex*), their heads, on seven-foot stems, clipped into spheres. My first idea had been to have them as a square allée, but I realized that as all else was square in the garden, a contrast of form was needed.

This garden, now known as the East Parterre, was where the 5th Marquess had removed the old patterned beds of box, gravel and polyanthus roses and made sixteen large square box-edged beds. In these I planted flowers and shrubs for all the seasons. In the spring they were filled with primroses and polyanthus, narcissus, early tulips, hepaticas, hellebores and euphorbias. Later, early irises, forget-me-nots, double wallflowers, May tulips and Scotch roses appeared. There was also one notable plant from the 5th Marquess' time, *Paeonia suffruticosa* 'Rock's Variety' (now called *P. rockii*), given to him by Sir Frederick Stern of Highdown fame, which stuns with the beauty of its huge white flowers with maroon-blotched centres against its dark leaves. For full summer, I planted many old-fashioned roses, lilies, peonies, irises, carnations and pinks, cistus, violas and pansies, and a plethora of English roses with their scented old-rose-like flowers and repeat flowering. For late summer and early autumn, there were old-fashioned small-flowered Michaelmas daisies looking like the mists of the season. In the centre of the beds were large box topiaries with concave sides facing the four corners, creating a more orderly structure to the plantings and a background for them. A guest remarked that they look like mitred bishops embracing their flock.

There was a great deal of gravel left. Wide paths made of a coarse kind of hoggin in a nasty gingery colour surrounded the whole garden and were exceedingly uncomfortable to the feet. The gravel was removed and was largely replaced by paving, with cobbled patterns here and there.

The height seemed all to be concentrated in the middle of the garden; tall and broad *Malus* 'John Downie', a lovely crab apple, but which here never seemed either to flower or fruit, dominated the centre ground, and there was no height at the sides. I left the malus for three years, but the longer they remained, the less I liked them. Having been given a chance to prove themselves, they had failed, so out they came and in went the *Quercus ilex*, which instantly seemed to provide a frame for the garden.

Opposite One of the two *Quercus ilex* walks in the East Parterre. The double lines of clipped mop-headed oaks provide an architectural frame for the garden.
Below In the East Parterre, looking south

I lined the walks beneath the holm oaks with fine Breedon Amber gravel, which, if well tamped and rolled down, is almost weed-proof and not picked up by the feet. Under the trees and in the gravel, I planted *Iris danfordiae*, a deliciously scented little yellow iris. Planted in the gravel the bulbs do not break up after flowering, never to flower again, as they do when planted in earth, and now they flower every year. I also planted *Oxalis enneaphylla*, which loved the gravel but appreciated the shade less. The borders under the walls on the east, north and south, which had previously held annuals, were all widened and planted with old roses, herbaceous peonies and tree peonies, and many other plants and bulbs for every season of the year. I had nowhere to plant the special small treasures that, if planted in borders, would be overwhelmed and disappear, never to be found again. Two corners that had been covered over with the horrid gravel gave the answer. Dug up and prepared with a good gritty mixture of soil and then a layer of fine grit to the depth of a couple of inches, they were ready for the species crocus, tulips and cyclamens, blue corydalis, baby irises and other precious alpines; the one corner in light shadow, the other in full sun.

My husband, who had a good eye for the architecture of a garden, had seen that the steps that led to the next terraces were too wide. This fault was disguised by planting yews (*Taxus baccata*), which grew into rounded columns, marching from just beyond the Italian wall fountain under the perron towards the far steps. At the same time, two of the square beds in front of the perron were halved diagonally to open up the space, and four stone early-eighteenth-century statues from the same villa in Italy were placed, two on either side of the steps to the second terrace and two facing each other north to south in the central grass walk.

There was still one important lack. There was nowhere to sit, to rest and look at what I hoped was going to be worth looking at. Stone bench seats seemed to be the answer and one more visit to the Italian stonemasons produced these. They were set in box (*Buxus sempervirens*) topiaried into comfortable embracing shapes to keep out the wind. I learned a tip from that inspired gardener Le Vicomte de Noailles, who put cork mats on his stone garden seats at the Villa Noailles to protect one from getting a damp bottom.

As a result of the war years and later neglect, the third Terrace, the one with the gigantic maze of yew, had fallen into a near disastrous state of disorder and decay, and it took fifteen years to get the yew into shape. I remember it being cut with sickle and stick, when it took many weeks to finish. Now, kept in shape by the extraordinary skill of Larry Laird with an electric hedge-trimmer, it has the precise lines of an architectural drawing and its annual trim is completed within three weeks.

The walk above the Maze was again gravel, as were the very wide paths running down either side. These were grassed down and the lavender hedge outlining the upper walk had to go too as the lavender looked peculiar against the grass. Instead, I planted tall box hedges with enclosures either end housing Lutyens oak seats found elsewhere on the estate. Eight huge stone urns, brought from Malta in the nineteenth century, were moved here from the outer South Court and planted with pyramidal Portugal laurels (*Prunus lusitanica* 'Myrtifolia').

Never far from my mind were the lists of plants Tradescant had used and his way of mingling flowers with fruit and even vegetables. There was a space between the box hedge and the retaining wall of the second terrace. I decided that sixteenth- and seventeenth-century plums, pears and apples, interspersed with the occasional climbing rose, should be fan-trained against the wall: one of the plums was grown

The East Parterre in spring. The light tones of the white tulips in the beds contrast with the darkness of the yew topiary and echo the pale blossom of the fruit trees in flower by the Maze.

Yew archways frame the apple walk in the Pool Garden.

at Fotheringay and romantically linked with Mary Queen of Scots during her imprisonment there. I had a vision of apple trees with their heads of clotted blossom being visible from the windows of the house in spring, so I planted them (grafted on free-growing stock) between the wall and the hedge and underplanted them with gold-laced polyanthus, which are happy in the light shade and moisture afforded by the trees.

To reach the next terrace, you walk down an avenue of apple trees. These I planted to run down on both sides of the Maze. They are made up of old varieties, some very old and probably grown in Tradescant's time. I underplanted them with varieties of *Crocus chrysanthus* in blues and creams for the spring when the trees are in blossom, and with oxeye daisies for when the trees are hung with fruit.

A swimming pool coloured a 'Californian' blue lay below a grass bank, looking brash and out of place. Moreover, the yew hedges were uncomfortably low with big gaps, so winds from every quarter could buffet and freeze the unfortunate bathers. The first thing was to fill the gaps and let the hedges grow high, encouraging the yew to form arches over all the entrances. In addition, having placed two Lutyens oak seats, one at either end of the pool, I planted curved yew hedges behind them, for greater shelter, and to give a more comfortable feel to the sitter than they might get from an open 'doorway' behind their back.

Cydonia oblonga, the common quince, was introduced to England by the Romans, and since John Tradescant brought it to Hatfield in 1611 it has been planted there in every century. It shows especially well when planted as a standard, with its large white rose-tinted flowers and scented golden fruit looking like something from a medieval tapestry. I planted four, two at either end of the pool, and in the centre of the crescent-shaped space on its eastern side a *Gleditsia triacanthos* 'Sunburst' given to me by a generous friend. The quinces are underplanted with *Limnanthes douglasii*, a fragrant hardy annual which is singularly labour-saving as it renews itself each year.

I saw this garden as a green space, quiet and peaceful, with the only flowers the apple and quince blossom and the only colour a touch of gold. And so it has come about. The Californian blue has vanished and on each of the four corners of the now tranquil-coloured pool stand Italian stone lemon pots planted with rosemary. The twelve-foot-high hedges are braced at intervals with clipped buttresses, while a beautifully carved stone statue by the sculptor Hamish Horsley surveys the scene from the centre of the yew hedge on the raised walk. Of course, as soon as the sun comes out, the tranquillity vanishes and the space echoes to the cries of happy bathers; but rarely are English summers warm for long.

The New Pond in May

There were many changes and much work to be done outside the formal gardens. The New Pond, possibly the site, or part of the site, of the Great Water Parterre designed in Robert Cecil's time by de Caus, was losing water through 'swallow' holes in its lining. The 4th Marquess, when he relined the pond, had employed a man and his son who came from Dorset and were the last people who knew how to make dew ponds, those mysterious 'scoops' on the Dorset downs that watered the animals grazing there. Father and son set to work, lined the pond with chalk from a nearby quarry and turned a herd of cattle into it. They fed them with straw, which throughout the winter they trampled into the chalk, making an impenetrable lining. We could only line it with blue clay, which we did, and hope for the best, our skilled adviser, Keith Wesley, warning us that there would always be the occasional swallow hole, which there has been – something to do with water finding its own level which I'm not sure I fully understand.

While the New Pond was empty, we discovered a rather interesting thing. There was strong evidence that it must have been relined about every fifty years. The whole area looked like a building site with this vast hole in the middle. The relining of the Pond gave us the perfect chance to do a little gentle landscaping round it.

But it was not until the hurricane winds in the autumn of 1987 and the January of 1988, when thirty-nine and then fifty-six major trees were lost in the gardens alone, that the wood on the rising ground above the eastern side of the Pond could be cleared. The major trees felled by the wind there included an ancient *Zelkova carpinifolia*, a majestic tree at least two hundred years old. It took two years to clear the garden, with the result that where before it was impossible to penetrate the thickets of thorns, nettles and brambles, the wood, which has come to be called Pond Wood, is now a place of delight, with its grassed woodland walk and young trees planted amongst the few remaining giants such as the two huge plane trees (*Platanus × hispanica*) introduced by Tradescant, and some fine beeches. Good has really come out of evil. I spent many a happy hour there planting cyclamens, wood anemones, hepaticas, dog's-tooth violets, snowflakes and snowdrops. Already there were carpets of *Narcissus pseudonarcissus*. Before the storms, there were a few poor strangled bluebells struggling for light; these seeded and spread in the dappled sun and freedom of the cleared woodland.

To create the New Pond, Robert Cecil had built a dam. Its northern side drops precipitously down, into what is known as the Dell. This name has not changed in four hundred years – it is frequently mentioned in the archives in papers dated 1610–12, notably one of 1611 from a Thomas Wilson to the Earl, describing how 'the Frenchman [almost certainly Salomon de Caus] means to make a force at the going out of the water from the island which but the current of the water shall drive up water to the top of the bank above the Dell and so descend into two fountains.' It is exciting and perhaps not too fanciful to think that this grand design has, though in a much more modest way, been reinterpreted in the Cascade and Pools I designed four hundred years later.

From the New Pond, many years ago, a large terracotta overflow pipe had been inserted into the wall of the dam, emerging on the other side. After heavy rains when the Pond was over-full, the water crashed down into the Dell and was lost in a ditch below. What a waste! Whenever I came to the Dell, my vision transformed the ugly pipe into a rocky hole with a rush of water cascading down the hill into a series of pools below. The years passed and my dream remained unfulfilled, with much other priority work to be done.

Then, in 2002, two things happened. I went to the Gainsborough exhibition at Tate Britain and saw there a small landscape of a waterfall cascading down into a succession of pools below and thence into a lake. I was transfixed. The landscape depicted a scene almost (minus the lake) exactly as I had imagined it for the Dell. I contacted my friend Karen Hearn at the Tate and she kindly sent me a photograph of the picture. The second was the discovery, on consulting our head gardener, Mr Beaumont, whose philosophy is 'anything can be done' and whose enthusiasm and energy for any new project is boundless, that he could find time to create the cascade. Picture in hand, we surveyed the site. Everything seemed to be possible and by 2004 the main elements were in place. Three pools, 12, 24 and 36 feet in diameter, were dug and lined with blue clay. They sloped slightly to the north and there were low weirs laid with slabs of stone which carried the water from pool to pool. There was a fourth circle, 48 feet wide, where a 5-foot canal of water surrounded grass in whose centre grew a *Quercus ilex* planted by the 5th Marchioness and now a shapely 50 feet high. It was, to an inch, exactly in the centre of the cascade. The northern boundary fence was moved back and Tamworth pigs

The Gainsborough Ponds in the Dell, fed by a cascade from the New Pond above

introduced to clear the ground of nettles, brambles and bracken and to manure it. And then it rained. It rained and rained, on and off, for weeks, and all our plans for the final cultivation of the site and the sowing of the grass seed before the winter set in had to be reluctantly postponed until the spring of 2005.

One of the major changes in the gardens was the abandonment of a twelve-acre kitchen garden. To visit it meant getting into a car and driving nearly half a mile. I had a time and motion study done which showed that we could lose seventy hours of working time in a week if there was bad weather and the gardeners had to walk that half-mile to work in the shelter of the greenhouse or potting shed. This did the trick and I was allowed to make the new kitchen garden. It faces full south with a brick wall on that side and tall whitethorn hedges on the other three. Whitethorn (*Crataegus laevigata* syn. *C. oxycantha*), which is studded with white scented flowers in May, was much used for hedges in the gardens of the sixteenth and seventeenth centuries. Because the ground slopes, the garden is on various levels, retained by brick walls and with steps for access. I made arched tunnels, with apples trained over them, leading to a small octagonal fountain surrounded by low clipped box. The stone figure in the centre of the fountain came from Italy and is of a naked child holding a fish, water flowing from the fish's mouth. There are arches with fruiting vines, and morello cherries were planted against the north wall and a potting shed and greenhouse erected. A narrow raised border where alpine strawberries are sometimes planted is the only place I know where you can pick them without getting backache.

With the move from the old kitchen garden, where there was a famous 'pear ground' (the Hatfield pears swept the board at the London fruit shows) and much other fruit, thought had to be given to where an orchard could be made. Luckily there was a spare piece of ground, an area entered from the Box Walk through a low seventeenth-century wrought-iron gate, which I had found in France in the 1980s. Enclosed by high beech hedges planted by the 5th Marchioness, it seemed to have no particular purpose and I thought it might admirably suit the planting of a small orchard. So it was roughly divided into squares by mown paths and planted with apples, pears, gage plums and cherries, mostly on dwarfing stock for ease of labour. This last was a mistake as the trees are more prone to disease on dwarf stock, something which we did not know at the time, and in 2003 they had all to be removed and replaced by half-standards.

In the orchard grass, I experimented with bulbs of *Narcissus* 'Hawera', to see if it would tolerate the thick grass. Happily it does and has spread with its pale yellow flowers, two or three to a stem, showing well in May, when the grass is not too high. I planted *Crocus chrysanthus* too, and a great many cowslips, and for late show *Camassia quamash* (syn. *C. esculenta*) with its sapphire-blue flowers.

I come now to the last garden on the eastern side of the house, known as the Mount Garden. It is described in the archives as having four mounts surrounding a bowling green. Two of the mounts have disappeared but there is one left, and half another, with a huge horse chestnut tree growing on it. Both were in a bad way, with their shape largely lost. Returfed and reshaped, one at least would, I hoped, become like the mount at Cranborne, 'a little hill to be scrambled up to view a fair prospect'. The prospect from the top of the greater mount is of the East Terrace, the East Parterre and the Great Court, or Outer Court, on the south of the house.

I made some other small alterations and additions to this garden. A pair of *Prunus avium* 'Plena' was planted, one on either side of the entrance to the Orchard through the beech hedge, and a wide flower and shrub border removed from below the eastern wall of the outer South Court, and the space grassed down. We planted *Arbutus menziesii* 'Marina' along the length of the wall. Tender when young, though hardy later, they had a harsh first winter and may not survive. On either side of the steps leading from the East Terrace, I made a small area of well-drained gritty soil for small treasures, where they would have the protection of the terrace walls. A honeysuckle and pale pink wisteria grow there, a rare climbing rose – 'Docteur Rouges' – and a flourishing *Myrtus communis*, grown in the sixteenth century and covered in white flowers in July and August.

In 1998, the work of removing the gravel from the South Court and West Terrace was begun. This, for me, was a significant and defining moment. My prime objective had always been to re-create, if at all possible, the intimacy between the house and its garden, which seemed, as far as my researches could discover, to have properly existed between the two when they were first made in 1611. The plan was to replace the gravel, and some York paving which the 5th Marquess had laid in the Inner Court some years earlier, by grass and Purbeck stone setts. Would this achieve the effect that we hoped for? That was the great question. The stone quarries in the Isle of Purbeck in Dorset were contacted and Mr Hayson of St Aldhelm's Quarry came to see us. He looked at the stone outside and inside the house and found that the steps to the doors in the Inner South Court were of Purbeck, as well as the footings of the supposedly Inigo Jones arcade. There were also paving stones of Purbeck in the basement of the house and Mr Harcourt Williams, our librarian, discovered in the archives a mention of a Purbeck stone path in the North Court.

It was logical that Robert Cecil should have used Purbeck stone. His manor house at Cranborne in Dorset was not far from Purbeck, and this stone, which was brought to London by boat up the Thames, was much used in the courtyards of the city and also at the royal palace of Hampton Court. I went to look at the courtyard at Hampton Court to see how the stones were laid and noted the way they ran in the paths that led to various doorways and entrances in the courts. I was impressed by the harmony between the soft red brick of the walls and the parchment colour of the stone, which had accumulated a certain amount of moss over the centuries.

The four garden houses were in a very poor state, most of them hardly safe to go into, as well as letting in damp and wet. They were put in order and, in 2004, their roofs were restored to their original shape, recorded in a dated drawing in the archives.

Next to be tackled was the redesigning of the Outer Court. I had always felt that the original level of the Court had been lower, with probably a stone ramp leading into the Inner Court – as is seen in a print of another Cecil house at Wimbledon – with the original height being on a level with the Park. This was proved to be so when the soil (which was largely rubble and stones) was removed, and the lower level was revealed to be topsoil. I would have much liked to have levelled the whole site, but this was impossible because it would have to have led to the dismantling of too much. A compromise had to be reached. When the soil had been extracted, broad grass walks were left surrounding the areas at a lower level. The central path divided the two matching areas and led to the great cast-iron gates erected in the nineteenth century. Banks three feet high were left below the raised walks. I planted, close against these, box (*Buxus sempervirens* 'Suffruticosa'), to form a hedge to grow till it reached the height of the brick openwork walls, built by the 2nd Marquess, which surrounded the site, so forming the raised walks which were typical features in gardens of the sixteenth and seventeenth centuries.

The view south over the
clipped evergreen designs of
the Outer Court and the great
cast-iron gates to the lime
avenue and the Park beyond

To fill the areas below the banks, I devised stylized patterns of clipped evergreens, four different designs surrounding simple circular pools, their edges flush with the grass, which contain fountains; their ten-foot-high jets falling into the water roughen its surface, making it difficult to see the golden koi carp which we introduced when Keith Wesley told me that they were kept in fish ponds and pools in the sixteenth and seventeenth centuries. I longed to do what Tsar Nicholas, the last Emperor of Russia, had done at Tsarskoe Selo, where the carp were tame and had little silver bells attached to them. When the Emperor and his family came to the fountains, there must have been a tinkling rush of sound as the fish swam up to be fed. What a delicious conceit and how the Elizabethans would have loved it! When the mutinous sailors from the ships at Yalta reached Tsarskoe Selo, they slaughtered the carp and stole their silver bells. Such a small barbaric act seems fittingly to signal the start of the seventy or so years of a great and bloody tyranny.

The four different designs for the clipped evergreens were a Tudor rose, oak leaves, a fleur-de-lys and a four-leaved shamrock. Oak leaves because they seemed to be typically of Hatfield, with its park and gardens full of ancient oak trees, including the oak under which Elizabeth was sitting when they rode down from London to tell her that she was Queen and the famous Lion Oak, which is supposed to be mentioned in the Domesday Book as being a remarkable size in 1066. The shamrock symbolizes my Irish family and good fortune, and the fleur-de-lys marks the life in France of the 3rd Marquess and our own. The Tudor rose needs no explanation.

My first idea was to plant evergreens in different tones of green, box, *Ilex crenata* and phillyrea, to be shaped and clipped in rounded forms, to look, I hoped, a little like veined green marble. The box, and to a lesser extent the phillyrea, flourished, but the ilex was a disaster. It did not like the heat and the summer after it was planted was a particularly hot one; nor did it seem to like the soil; and in spite of feeding and watering, it did not thrive and had to be removed.

On either side of the central paved path leading to the great nineteenth-century cast-iron gate, I placed square artificial stone containers (by Blashfields of Stamford), each planted with a standard holm oak (*Quercus ilex*). They had been for many years standing empty in the middle of the arches in the arcade of the South Front.

I always feel a house should be enveloped with plants that look good all the year round, therefore largely evergreen and ever-grey, many preferably scented. The obvious ones, of course, are the homely rosemary and lavender, but there are several others, such as the sages, thymes and daphnes and *Choisya* 'Aztec Pearl'. In the borders round the house I planted some of these, interspersed by the occasional tree peony, dwarf flag iris and many roses. In the spring, there are bulbs, tulips and, for later in the season, lilies. One day, I had a fancy to do something completely different and decided to have only black and white plants and flowers around the house. Apart from some roses on the walls, nearly everything was already white. The black was more tricky, but the search for it was fun and nearly completed in 2004 when I left Hatfield. Two more *Magnolia denudata* grow on the south walls of the wings between the towers and sometimes the first flowers are peering through my windows by the end of February.

To complete the sense of enclosure round the house, we planted yew hedges on the east and west, running from the corners of the East and West Towers of the wings to the corners of the garden houses. High wrought-iron gates in the yew completed this sense of enclosure.

A mown path through the
the Wilderness, with a crab
apple in flower on the left

When we did the new planting in what is now called the Wilderness we had to contend with not only the foundations of the old Conservatory but those of the Hothouse and the Ivy House as well, not to speak of the concrete platforms where Nissen huts were built during the Second World War when the house was a military hospital. I believe some of the trees that we planted may not have grown well because their roots have come up against some of those remains. Carrying on with my vendetta against the hoggin gravel, I grassed down the paths in the Wilderness and laid out a rough herringbone pattern of grass paths, with new-planted trees defining them, mowing roundabouts round the ancient trees (and some of the younger ones) that came in the centre of the paths.

The 5th Marquess and Marchioness had planted many rhododendrons and azaleas (as well as some kalmias, pernettias and pieris). The soil was not ideal for them and they did not thrive. I removed some of the least happy ones and the rather violent purple, red and orange hybrids. Luckily the prettiest seem the happiest, especially the pale scented azaleas with flowers like honeysuckle and the great white scented rhododendron that flowers very late. *R. augustinii* is pretty too, and there is a group looking well at the top of the Wilderness when the bluebells are in flower. Here and there amongst the forest trees, I planted *Prunus avium*, A.E. Housman's 'loveliest of trees'. I planted groups of birch too, their chalk-white stems underplanted with snowdrops and hellebores; and on either side of one of the main grass paths is an informal avenue of *Acer japonicum*, all grown from a batch of unnamed seedlings. Young as they are, they already make their mark in the autumn when their leaves turn.

A *Davidia involucrata*, the pocket handkerchief tree, discovered in China by the French missionary Père David in 1869, was planted by the 5th Marchioness in the 1960s. It had never flowered. It is a greedy feeder, and I was told to pile on the manure every autumn, which I did. Still no flowers. So one day, walking in the Wilderness, I went up to it and told it that if it didn't flower the next year, I would cut it down. I know this is hard to believe but the following May it put forth one flower and each year since it produces more. I planted many white camellias to join the pink ones planted by the 5th Marquess, which are now huge bushes. Eucryphias flourished for late summer flowering and there are species roses for May. Sheets of *Crocus tommasinianus* and other crocuses flower in early spring, followed by primroses and cowslips grown from seed, which are spreading far and wide. Cuckoo-pint and wild orchids are beginning to appear, as, since 1972, the long grass, before then cut in June, is not cut until late July or early August, depending on the season, so the seeds of the bulbs and wild flowers have time to ripen and fall. The grass in most of the Wilderness is coarse and long, as in other areas of the gardens where it is not mown closely. To reduce its height and thickness, we planted yellow rattle, which is a parasite on the roots of grasses. It is a pretty wild flower with yellow blossom, and magical in its effect on coarse grass, reducing it in height and thickness, so allowing new wild flowers to appear.

Magnolias do well, and I planted quite a few. *Magnolia* × *loebneri* 'Merrill', *M.* × *soulangeana* – a group of seven – and *M.* × *s.* 'Alba', as well as *M. campbelli* subsp. *mollicomata*, for which you need to have patience, as it takes ten to fifteen years to flower. Why didn't I begin all my operations in the gardens by planting trees, hedges and screens to hide the boundary fences? It was foolish not to and I've regretted my stupidity ever since, especially when I contemplate little trees six to twelve feet high when I could be looking at giants thirty years old.

The hurricane winds of 1987 and 1988 devastated the Wilderness near the house. Mr Beaumont remembers being woken by the roar of the wind. He dressed to go and see if the greenhouse was all

right, but the force of the tempest was such that he could not get out of his front door to take a step forward. Heavy thuds and crashes marked the fall of forest giants. I heard the same depressing sounds, and the noise of the tornado was as though an express train was coming into the house.

What a mournful scene met us the next morning! The north end of the Wilderness had lost the greatest number of its ancient trees. After two years of clearing and making good the site, the replanting began. The new trees have not grown particularly well. There is no great depth of soil there and it is anyway rather stony and poor. Gravel over London clay, with an occasional patch of something better, plus rare outbreaks of chalk, is what we had in the 45 acres of garden, and we had to make the best of it, which was hard work, though things were easier in the flower gardens because we built up the fertility of the soil with organic fertilizers such as fish, blood and bone, calcified seaweed and large quantities of the homemade compost which came to be known as the 'Hatfield Pudding'.

The planting of the Hornbeam Walk was the first part of what was to become the second of my Hatfield swan songs. It was to lead to a pair of stone steps which would take you, if you turned right, to the tall wrought-iron gates, standing between brick pillars with stone spheres on them, which lead into the Scented Garden. Between the columnar hornbeams I planted *Iris reticulata* and *Tulipa batalinii*, 'Lilac Wonder', which increased in spite of being in a thick carpet of grass.

If you should turn to the left at the end of this allée, you would find yourself in an avenue of *Malus* 'John Downie'. They are very lovely in the spring, with thick white blossom, and in the autumn with large red fruits. I planned to do something new here. This was to complete the walk from the southwest Garden House down the hornbeam avenue, which framed it, into the Holly Walk. It was going to need rather careful planning and planting, as I felt it must not look like a flower garden because it was fringing the Wilderness. I planted tall box plants to form eventually an archway over the pair of steps and another facing it across the path. Huge plants of box planned to be clipped into billowing forms lead on the right and left from the entrance gate to the malus avenue. A paved path forms a narrow border on your right, under the fifteenth-century brick wall of the Scented Garden. On your left, there are four large beds divided by short paved paths, the central one leading into another narrow avenue, this time of limes. More huge box bushes were planted to form an informal hedge, likewise clipped in billowing fashion which I hoped would give a certain purposeful sense of enclosure and a more gradual transition from the planted beds into the wild. Again, purposefully, I planted these with woodland lilies, small-flowered species peonies and roses such as *Rosa × odorata*, some hostas, heucheras and a *Viburnum* f. *tomentosum*, and planned to plant some woodland bulbs as well as less sophisticated climbers on the wall. There are already many hellebores, and some *Fritillaria pallidiflora* which seem to be very happy.

At the end of this walk, another pair of stone steps takes you into the Holly Walk. This is a curious place, which has seen a few changes since it was planted in the nineteenth century. It was first made by the 3rd Marquess. He was then both Prime Minister and Foreign Secretary and found it difficult to get any exercise for his eighteen-stone frame. The Walk was laid with asphalt and a holly hedge planted either side and it ran the full length of the 200-foot Conservatory to the wall of the Royal Palace Yard beyond. Here, as well as on narrow asphalt paths he had had laid all over the Park, the Prime Minister took his exercise, riding a tricycle. A boy perched on the back with his hands on the Prime Minister's shoulders, ready to jump off and open the gates for him.

By the 1970s, the asphalt was much decayed and full of weeds and was not a pretty sight. However, my husband had happy memories of roller skating on it with his brothers and viewed it with much sentiment, so it was a while before it was swept away and put down to grass. Several more years passed and then, in 2002, the moment came when it could be tackled. It needed a good deal of shaping up, as in some places it was one width and in some another, the hedges bulged forward or recessed back and the grass walk was not level. I visualized it as a quiet green space, a contrast to, and a retreat from, the flower gardens, their colour and their busy-ness and activity. It should, I thought, be strictly architectural. It was then that I remembered the Borromini Gallery in Perspective which I had seen many years ago in the Spada Palace in Rome. Cardinal Bernardino Spada, who delighted in Baroque virtuosities, asked the architect Borromini to design it. It was built in a year, in 1652, in collaboration with the Augustinian mathematician Giovanni Maria di Bitonto. The real measurement of the Gallery is 8.82 metres, but it has a virtual depth of 35 metres. The optical illusion is created by the convergence of the planes of the colonnade and the ground slope of the floor towards the vanishing point. Four or five years of growth will be needed to shape the pillars, their capitals and bases and the hedges themselves before the right effect is achieved in the Holly Walk. Fanciful? Yes, and not exactly a Gallery in Perspective, but inspired by one.

The Walk is now edged with stone and at the south end is the vast head of Queen Elizabeth I in artificial stone. She had sat on the roof ever since being brought from the façade of the old Royal Exchange in London, which was rebuilt in 1825 after a fire. We had a plinth made for her, and now she broods in stately splendour not far from where she spent her girlhood.

A high wrought-iron gate leads from the Holly Walk into the Scented Garden. This was the first flower garden that I redesigned, beginning it in the mid-seventies. If an integrated design was to be achieved here, much had to be altered. The royal palace had been on the main road from the north to London and almost certainly the broad path running from the great oak gate, with a postern in it, to the wrought-iron gate in the south in this garden was part of that road. This road, or path, had the usual hoggin gravel on it, which, when removed, was replaced by the Breedon Amber and edged either side with York paving, the uneven edges facing into the centre. On one side was a broad border backed by a wall. This wall must have been the west wall of the Privy Garden – which we know about from a plan of it in the archives – protecting it from the London road. Unfortunately, in the nineteenth century it was much reduced in height, but its lower half has the original Tudor bricks. The garden is enclosed by two other sixteenth-century walls on the north and south, and on the west by the hedge lining the Holly Walk; all of them had broad borders in front of them. The beautiful walls were largely hidden by huge shrubs and the border below the hedge was on a slope and came for no obvious reason well beyond the bottom step of the stone stairs leading to the Holly Walk. There was a great deal of bedding out and in the centre of the garden were two huge *Malus* 'John Downie' which looked very out of place. I took a deep breath and removed them. Then I pushed back the sloping east-facing border to the line of the steps, which meant it became a raised border faced by a retaining wall of brick. I had the two other borders divided in half lengthways by narrow York stone paths and subdivided from back to front by a broader middle path and two narrow ones. Now you could see the beautiful Tudor brick walls and see and smell the plants growing on them. *Azara serrata* and *Trachelospermum jasminoides* thrive on the north-facing wall, while *Cytisus battandieri* with its scent of pineapple and *Clematis rehderiana*, smelling like cowslips, grow with other scented wall plants on the one facing south.

At the heart of this garden is the Herb Garden, enclosed by a hedge of clipped sweetbrier, *Rosa rubiginosa*, the eglantine of poetry and medieval tapestry and illustration. It has a delicious fruity smell, like ripe apples. Several of its hybrids are grown with it, including the double marbled sweetbrier, which is irresistibly charming. Paved paths lead to a sundial surrounded by a circle of chamomile, and with thyme planted at its foot. All the paths, paved at their edges, originally had chamomile planted in their centres but the feet of thousands of visitors were too much for it to bear and it had to be replaced by Breedon gravel.

The cook has a long but rather agreeable walk through the garden to where I planted the herbs, a collection of everything that she might need for her soups and sauces, sweets and meats. The mints, which walk everywhere, were planted in bottomless containers to control their wandering roots. The main beds in the Herb Garden were edged with parsley, which rather unexpectedly grows like a low hedge, its colour a vivid emerald green, a colour unlike any other plant I know.

There are four pieces of lawn on either side of the Herb Garden, divided by paved edged paths. These have their centres planted with grass, and pass through high box hedges with *oeilles de boeuf* (peepholes) giving a view into the garden. The four paths lead you under clipped arches of box, into circular green bowers, the box rising over a frame. Four panels are open to the sky, four closed by box, but it will be several years yet before the bowers have grown enough to complete the vision I had of them in 1997: places of sun and shadow, of quiet contemplation, where you could sit on one of the four stone benches, write a poem and listen, as the simple jet drops water into the bowl below, and the box, on a sunny day, lightly pervades the air with its musky, dusky scent.

This is a garden crammed full of a thousand different scents: scents of shrubs and trees, scents springing from flower and foliage, bulb or tuber. There are scents produced in every season. Even in the depths of winter there is sweet bay (*Sarcococca hookeriana* var. *humilis*), clipped as a low hedge and scenting the air for yards around in February, and the wintersweet (*Chimonanthus fragrans*) with its pale yellow waxy flowers marked with ox-blood red. Then in spring there are the plums and the intensely sweet flowers of silver-leaved *Elaeagnus commutata*, and the sweet-smelling tulips 'Prince of Orange' and 'Prince of Austria', auriculas and primroses, the sweet violet, and of course daphnes. Then lilies, *Lilium regale* and *L. auratum*, lilies-of-the-valley and sweet geraniums, every one with a different scent – spice, peppermint or rose, or a scent uniquely its own. There are white Guernsey stocks grown from seed gathered in Guernsey itself and its purple sister known as the 'Guernsey Violet'; the white one I have planted like a hedge, either side of one of the paved entrance paths. The broad west-facing border I divided (either side of the main entrance into the Scented Garden from the Privy Garden), by making paths leading to seats, planted in their centres with many different scented thymes, which have a difficult time surviving the visitors' feet. In this border, as in many of the others, there are also old-fashioned roses, the Damasks, Gallicas and Centifolias, as well as scented roses for the walls, and the English roses, bred by David Austin, which look like the old ones and smell as sweet, but flower till the first frosts. A pair of standard quince trees on either side of the main entrance is hung in the autumn with deliciously scented golden fruit which remind me, rather nonsensically, of the nursery rhyme 'I had a little nut tree and nothing would it bear,/ But a silver nutmeg and a golden pear', for golden pears are what they look like.

In the north-east corner of the garden, a flight of stone steps takes you into the Privy Garden. As you climb them, to your left, a bothy-cum-toolshed forms, with the walls, a warm corner. The pretty rose 'Climbing Pompon de Paris' grows near the door and on the other side *Lonicera fragrantissima*, covered with sweetly scented cream flowers in late winter and spring. There was, on the right of the steps, when I first saw the garden, a horrid kind of rockery set with what I believe are called 'pudding stones', made of small pebbles stuck in lumps of cement. Not pretty and not improved by a planting of rather tired old yuccas. Removed as soon as possible, it was replaced by narrow terraces faced with brick, filled with gritty soil and chippings, and planted with scented alpines and bulbs and a wonderful-smelling *Muscari macranthum* with huge yellow and purple flowers. It came from Kew, and was given me by my friend Sir George Taylor, then the Director. Against one of the pillars of this entrance to the garden is a very old plant of lemon verbena (*Aloysia triphylla* syn. *Lippia citriodora*). It is tender and has to be wrapped up in several layers of bracken and sacking each winter.

Above the Scented Garden lies the Privy Garden – now the West Parterre. A plan of this, dated 1608, exists in the archives, and in the 1900s Lady Gwendolen Cecil used ideas from its design when she

The vista between the north and south entrances in the West Parterre, with the stone fountain and central pool

created her parterre. At the centre of the parterre is a large fountain, planted with waterlilies, and in it there are golden and silver koi carp. The fountain is not, sadly, one of those designed by Salomon de Caus, but the octagonal centre basin is very old and could be one of his.

There was a great deal of bedding done in this parterre, and there were many harsh-coloured modern roses. The soil was stony and poor and the patterns of the beds were somewhat lost. We dug and fed and replanted and at the same time allowed the hedge to increase in height to give more secrecy and shelter. The corners of the hedge at either side of each of the four entrances were allowed to grow enough to be clipped into finials and the four corners of the yew hedge to rise, forming snug enclosures with stone benches from Italy on platforms of brick, and a clipped yew sphere on the hedge behind them. Many new plants were introduced here and many of the labour-intensive bedding plants eliminated, although quite a number of old favourites have been kept. There was room for tall things here like sunflowers and hollyhocks, some of the taller David Austin roses, *Euphorbia characias* and *E.c.* subsp. *wulfenii*. I tried to have colour and form here at each season and in early spring there are, amongst other things, clusters of *Iris reticulata*, as well as species tulips, *Euphorbia amygdaloides*, polyanthus, ipheion, sometimes called triteleia, and perennial wallflowers. These are followed by many tulips in early May with peonies, iris and the main flowering of the roses and lilies, to be followed, as summer fades, by the last of the roses, late lilies, Michaelmas daisies and alstroemerias.

Outside the yew hedge there are lawns and at each corner is a mulberry tree, one of them said to be the last of those supposedly planted by James I on his visit to the house. I replanted the other three, and made octagonal wooden seats to go around them, and propagated King James's tree. A walk

surrounding this garden on four sides is covered by a canopy of pleached lime (*Tilia × europaea*), of unknown age, but thought to have been planted in the late eighteenth century. The walks under the limes – more of the 3rd Marquess's paths for exercising on his tricycle – were covered in black asphalt. It was exceedingly ugly, cracked and weedy and the whole garden perked up when it was removed and the pretty Breedon Amber gravel was laid. At the sides of the Lime Walk in spring there are sheets of violet and white crocus, *Anemone blanda*, *A.b.* 'White Splendour', and *A. appennina*, as well as *A. coronaria* and *A.* De Caen Group, double and single white-flowered forms. They are supposed to be tender but are happy in the grass and come up year after year, and an unknown white saxifrage has spread generously amongst them. Under the wall of the West Terrace, I made a narrow border. Here there is broken shade, and cream, white and green hellebores grow sturdily with woodruff and white primroses, *Dodecatheon meadia* f. *album* (first introduced in the early eighteenth century) and a small-flowered white vinca, with white- flowered heucheras, a variegated Solomon's seal, snow- drops and a white *Puschkinia scilloides*.

This small piece of the garden I find that rare and happy thing, almost entirely satisfactory. I say almost because only if the West Terrace were three feet lower would it be perfect.

Walking out of the Lime Walk northwards and looking to the right, you see a low nineteenth-century cast-iron gate, which is the entrance from the North Court into the West Gardens. On your left as you enter, I made a raised bed faced with bricks. There is a tall yew tree growing here and two of the tallest and finest *Phillyrea angustifolia* trees I have ever seen. There are another two at the entrance to the East Gardens from the North Court. They must be nearly a hundred and fifty years old, with fine trunks and

The West Parterre, with, beyond, the Scented Garden and the Holly Walk

Standard medlars (*Mespilus germanica*) and a walnut tree (*Juglans regia*) appear as decorative features beside the ancient horse chestnut (*Aesculus hippocastanum*), with its candle-like flowers, which dominates this restful green area of the West Garden. Elegantly shaped box hedges line the paths, while yew hedging encloses eighteenth-century Italian statuary and creates a bower for a wooden seat.

heads of evergreen foliage looking almost fashionably cloud-pruned. It is rare to see a tall phillyrea tree even in its countries of origin, North Africa and Southern Europe, but in sixteenth- and seventeenth-century England it was often used for hedges. Indeed, the seventeenth-century diarist John Evelyn recommended it as a hedge plant.

We are now in a quite large area of flat ground furnished with lawn and Breedon gravel paths, trees, statues and seats. There is an immense horse chestnut tree (*Aesculus hippocastanum*) with a wooden octagon seat around it. This chestnut is a native of the region between Greece and Albania and was introduced into England in the seventeenth century. It is a beautiful sight in May when it is covered with candles of white flowers. A walnut tree planted by the 5th Marchioness grows in front of the yew hedge looking south. You sit on the seat beside it and you have a view down the Lime Walk to the stone steps leading to the Hornbeam Walk. Another path to the east leads to a long wooden seat half-hidden by the box and yew clipped in a bower around it. All the paths are framed by box hedges. Now four and a half feet high, they are curved down, rising at each of the corners into shaped finials, which are not yet fully grown but will, eventually, have small spheres on their tops. The main path leading to the chestnut tree has a row of standard medlar trees behind the box hedges that frame it. The medlars, a graceful umbrella shape, have large white flowers in the spring, and they are laden with fruit later in the year.

Against the yew hedge facing west are four early-eighteenth-century stone statues which came from the same villa near Lake Como as those in the East Parterre. I let the yew form niches around them, which will give the eye something perpendicular to rest on against the rather monotonous horizontals of the rest of the hedge, and at the same time frame the statues.

This part of the West Garden lies above the garden of the palace where Queen Elizabeth lived as a girl. So I thought to keep the planting here to trees grown at that period; a row of *Prunus rhexii*, a flowering and fruiting cherry planted by the Elizabethans, went in along the yew hedge which faced south, and very lovely they are in the spring. Mulberries were planted above the palace's knot garden. In the 1990s, Hatfield and Villandry, the magnificent château in France with its famous gardens of much the same period, were 'twinned' one with t'other, and the Fruiterers' Company marked this historic event with the ceremonial planting of a gift of mulberry trees. A similar ceremony was carried out at Villandry.

I had for several years much wanted to create a garden in front of the Old Palace and plant it with the flowers grown in the time of the Tudors, and those grown and collected by the Tradescants. In 1982, there was the opportunity to do so. All that remained of the Old Palace was the Great Hall, with the Upper and Lower Solar rooms, plus a few rooms to the north. Robert Cecil had pulled down the other three sides of the palace, leaving high banks framing what must have been the inner courtyard of the building. It was here that I wanted to create the garden.

The 5th Marchioness had made here a simple garden of a border planted with old-fashioned roses, a central round pond and four squarish areas of grass formed by paths paved in York stone. In each of the four grass spaces was a *Malus* 'John Downie', underplanted with *Scilla siberica*. We can only guess what the area was like before the demolition of the three wings which had enclosed it, but most probably it was paved, though perhaps there could have been a simple garden for herbs.

The first thing I did was to study the books in the library at Hatfield on gardens, gardening and plants of the period. Thomas Hill's *The Gardener's Labyrinth* of 1579 was one of them, William Lawson's *New Orchard and Garden* (1618) another, and there were others, such as Estienne's *Agriculture et Maison Rustique* (1594) with designs of knots. I looked at the knot garden at All Souls' College, Oxford, that at Jesus College and the one at Beauregard, near Blois, not to speak of knot designs on Celtic crosses, in stone carvings and on wood panelling (there are several examples at Hatfield), plus those in embroidery of the period. There is even a knot in an embroidered binding worked by the eleven-year-old Princess Elizabeth on a book she gave as a present to Katherine Parr. Perhaps it was embroidered when she was at Hatfield. Out of all this study and research came not only a greater knowledge of the history of gardening in the period, but the plans for the Knot Garden at Hatfield.

Knots were beds laid out in formal elaborate patterns, the geometrical lines being planted with low clipped evergreens, such as germander, winter savory, santolina, thrift or box. There were closed knots, when the open spaces left by the interlacing, intertwining or geometric patterns of the closely clipped hedges were filled with flowers, or were entirely filled by the interweaving hedges; and open knots which, to give variety of tone, had the spaces filled with different-coloured earths, brick dust, or even ashes – or, according to Gervase Markham, flowers of one colour.

With the Wars of the Roses came discontent and disorder, and it was not till the first of the Tudors came to the throne in 1485 that there was a revival of orderly gardening, though quite early in the fifteenth century the knotted bed had begun to take the place of the simple rectangle of previous years. With the abandonment of defences under the secure rule of the Tudors and the development of the Tudor style, an elaborate formal layout for the garden evolved which was to be maintained for some two centuries.

The *Hypnerotomachia* by Franceso Colonna was to have a powerful influence on the gardens of the Elizabethan and Jacobean periods. The English translation appeared in 1592, nearly a hundred years after it was published in Venice. It was the story of a lover's search for his beloved through a dreamland of architectural fantasies, classical ruins and gardens filled with elaborate topiary work, statues and flower beds, laid out in patterns. Colonna's dreamy vision of a Golden Age appealed to Elizabethan and Jacobean society, which delighted in symbolism, threads that led them back to classicism and a revived interest in chivalry and the courtly acts. There was a facsimile copy of the book in the library at Hatfield.

The knot was the central feature of all gardens of pleasure in the sixteenth century and it has one outstanding merit: it is an object of beauty and interest the whole year round, at its best perhaps in spring, but almost as effective and doubly welcome in winter.

And what of the flowers that were planted in knots? Nothing is more characteristic of this age than its love of flowers, a taste that can develop only when primary wants are satisfied and life is reasonably secure. The increased trading activities overseas brought about the introduction of new plants, plants like the oriental hyacinths, the ranunculus, columbine and Star of Bethlehem; and at the same time the Huguenot weavers, fleeing from the massacres of St Bartholomew's Day, brought over a number of exotic plants that were ideally suited to the small enclosed beds, including auriculas, pinks, primroses, violets, double daisies and thrift.

Also in the fifteenth and sixteenth centuries, a great many of the English wild flowers were used with, as we have seen, occasional rare plants brought by travellers from abroad, but as trade increased and travel widened, 'outlandish flowers' began to arrive in ever increasing numbers: tulips, the Catalonian jasmine, anemones, *Dianthus* – 'the open knots', says Parkinson, 'are more proper for these.'

The Elizabethans loved symbolism, the strange, the bizarre and fanciful. They liked the striped and variegated, the double flowers, the green flowers, the great rose plantain, hose-in-hose primroses, Jacks-in-the-green, and this taste for oddities and the unusual was carried on into the seventeenth century. Here is William Lawson writing in his *New Orchard and Garden*, published in 1618, of 'the Rose red, Damask, Velvet, and double, double Province Rose; the sweet Musk Rose, double and single, the double and single white rose, the fair and sweet scenting woodbine, double and single and double double; purple cowslips and double cowslips and double double cowslips; primrose double and single. The violet nothing behind the rest for smelling sweetly. A thousand more will provoke your content, and all these by the skill of your gardener, so comely and orderly placed in your borders and squares and so intermingled that on looking thereon we cannot but wonder to see, what Nature corrected by Art can do.'

Nature corrected by Art – that surely is the perfect description of a knot garden and the formal, clipped, topiaried gardens of Tudor and Stuart England.

The court of the Old Palace seemed the ideal frame for a knot garden. It had high banks on three sides, so it could be looked down upon, which the knot gardens of the fifteenth and sixteenth centuries ideally were. It had water, was beautifully sheltered and did not seem to be a frost pocket. The creation of this garden was going to be fun, and I looked forward to it with keen anticipation.

The first thing was to draw a plan. There were to be three knots and a foot maze, or labyrinth. Labyrinths, which may have originated in Crete or Egypt, featured in Tudor gardens as a relic of the Middle Ages.

There are mazes on the floors of cathedrals and churches where sinful man, penitent, crawled round the labyrinth on his knees saying prayers at various stations on the way. Sometimes they were used as an alternative to going on a pilgrimage to the Holy Land, and were thought of as symbolizing man's journey through life, when, after traversing a tortuous and difficult path, he would finally reach Paradise.

At first glance, the court seemed to be square but measurement proved it otherwise, and when three square knots and a square labyrinth were fitted into the area, several empty spaces were left. These I filled with two long beds edged with winter savory (*Satureja montana*), and with the grey *Santolina chamaecyparissus* in the centres. In the other empty spaces, I put round beds, two each side of the entrance to the palace, and planted a silver and golden variegated holly, topiaried in layers and underplanted with *Vinca minor* f. *alba* and *Scilla siberica*. The hedges of the knots and the labyrinth were of box, the plants being grown from thousands of cuttings raised in sand in 1979 and planted finger-sized in 1981, their root system much larger than their stem and leaf.

There were borders under the very low brick wall which had been the base of an openwork one, put in by the 2nd Marquess in particularly ugly mauvish Victorian brick backed by a hoggin gravel path. We removed both borders and wall and planted whitethorn (*Crataegus laevigata* syn. *C. oxyacantha*), which was much used for clipped hedges in the fifteenth and sixteenth centuries, and we topiaried finials either side of the entrances to the garden. Old, probably seventeenth-century, bricks found on the estate were used to lay all the paths except the main cross paths. These, which are of York stone, had been put in by the 5th Marquess. They led to a round pond, which I turned into a fountain with a limestone basin on a baluster supporting a single jet of water. In the paved circle around the fountain we put copies of Elizabethan terracotta pots, with a trellis pattern, which we planted with old varieties of clove carnations. There were now grass paths behind the whitethorn hedges at the bottoms of the grass banks, and at the top of the banks a low wooden trellis fence, which surrounded the whole garden, its posts crowned by wooden balls. These were coconut-shy balls found in a shop in Southampton!

The hard landscaping of the garden was now complete, and the treasure hunt for the plants began. Although the palace was built in the late fifteenth century, I decided not to be too purist and limit myself to plants of that date, because I wanted also to include a collection of the plants introduced by the Tradescants and those grown up to 1700. Their colours, form and character seemed to look right, and to harmonize with the architecture and setting they grew in. Besides, many were rare and precious and needed to be in a place where they could be kept an eye on and, if necessary, propagated.

There were several people who gave me expert advice and shared with me their deep knowledge and experience in growing plants of these periods (not to speak of their generous gifts of the plants themselves) for which I shall always be grateful.

One was Roy Genders, whose books I had read and found to be a mine of precious information about early plants still surviving in gardens, their history and where they might be found. I was lucky enough to enjoy his delightful company on the several occasions he came to Hatfield to see the gardens, but more especially to talk about the plants grown in the gardens of Tudor and Stuart England, the florists' flowers, and those found in cottage gardens, many of which had survived in these gardens from the earliest times of their introduction, thanks to the cottagers faithfully propagating them from seeds and cuttings over the years. Among them were plants like the ancient pinks, the hose-in-hose cowslips and double primroses. Brian Halliwell, at Kew, was another erudite plantsman and botanist who came to see

the garden while I was planting it and helped me greatly with his expertise and knowledge of early plants. Michael Hoog, who had a nursery in Haarlem where he grew rare and wonderful bulbs, many of which he had raised himself or found in the wild, also came to the garden and it was through him that the Hortus Bulborum in Holland sent me a collection of historic tulips and narcissus to grow there, including the swan-necked daffodil and the pink and white tulip 'Lac van Rijn' dating from 1620. These were all exciting acquisitions and added greatly to the interest in the garden.

John Harvey, with encyclopaedic knowledge of early plants, fruit and trees, produced a small book which was the inspiration of Maureen Taylor, the manager of our garden centre at Cranborne, listing all these plants with the descriptions of them and their dates of introduction. This was a great help to me, as were my several visits to him and his wife at their home in Somerset.

Of course, the heat and burden of the day fell on the broad shoulders of Mr Beaumont and his team, who carried out the construction of the garden and its planting in an impressively short time. It was begun in 1979 with the striking of box cuttings, and finished in 1982. The paths had been laid and the beds edged with bricks and the main planting had been completed. Remembering how much the Tudors and Elizabethans loved the bizarre and the fanciful, the striped, and the variegated, I planted the hedgehog holly and the plant like the skin of a snake, *Dracunculus vulgaris*, the dragon arum or snakeplant, its leaves flesh-coloured with black, also the rose root (*Rhodiola rosea*), hose-in-hose primroses, auriculas and double primroses, the great rose plantain with its green double leaf-like flowers and the plume hyacinth, as well as very many less eccentric plants, or plants not eccentric at all, like the Madonna lily, and the forget-me-not, which was the personal emblem of Henry of Lancaster, afterwards Henry IV, who wore it believing that those who did would never be forgotten.

I planted lavender, of course, which reached England with the Romans. William Lawson said that it was 'Good for bees', while Parkinson told us that 'It would pierce the senses . . . to comfort, and would dry up the moisture of a cold brain.' One hopes it worked. Irises went in too, *germanica*, *pallida* and 'Florentina', also *Lilium chalcedonicum* with scarlet Turk's cap flowers which grew wild in the fields beyond Constantinople and was grown in every Tudor garden.

Candytuft, hyssop, thymes, *Matthiola longipetala* subsp. *bicornis* – the Elizabethan gardeners' night violet, with its delicious night-time scent – then gillofers or gillyflowers, which we call stocks. Hellebores too, and *Lychnis chalcedonica*, which was brought back by pilgrims at the time of the Crusades, with its tiny petals forming a scarlet cross, its English name being cross of Jerusalem. I planted as many of the pinks grown in those early times as I could find. Some were elusive, but as interest in them has grown over the last years, several have been rediscovered, including 'Nonsuch', 'Painted Lady' and 'Green Eyes' or 'Musgrave's Pink'.

Many bulbs were planted too, the Scottish crocus (*Crocus biflorus*), *Erythronium dens-canis*, *Colchicum autumnale* and snowdrops amongst them. Over the four bowers I had made, and set against the hedges facing north and south, I planted the sweetbrier (*Rosa rubiginosa*), the honeysuckle *Lonicera periclymenum*, and jasmine, which was first introduced in 1528, and used to form scented places to rest.

Roses of course, I planted in abundance. Many, such as the Gallicas and Albas, can be traced back to classical times. The Damask roses were grown by the Persians, the Crusaders bringing them back to Europe, and Parkinson, in 1629, grew twelve different varieties. 'Alba Maxima' seems indestructible. It has lived for centuries in the gardens of castles and cottages, and smells delicious, its flowers blush pink,

The Old Palace with its Knot Garden and the fountain of the golden boy with his moving wing and sounding trumpet

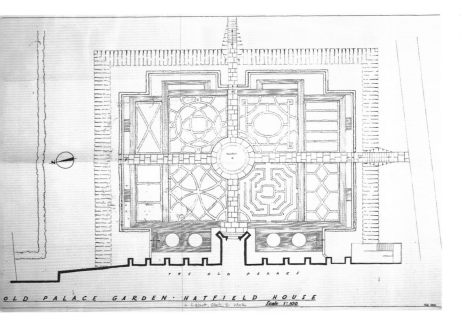

OLD PALACE GARDEN · HATFIELD HOUSE

turning to creamy white and 'double-double'. 'Alba Semiplena' was the white rose of York and then there is 'Maiden's Blush', called by the French 'Cuisse de Nymphe' or 'La Séduisante', names which give one a clue to its seductive beauty. *Rosa × centifolia*, the old cabbage rose, grown certainly before 1600, is double-double too, and a *rose des peintres* – Redouté being one of the artists who painted it. A delicious little rose, a Gallica, 'Burgundiaca', the Burgundy rose, only three feet high, with tiny flowers and leaves, I planted too. It is known to have been introduced before 1664. And the apothecary's rose, *R. gallica* var. *officinalis*, which has a romantic history. It is thought that the King of Navarre, who calls it in a poem 'the rose from the land of the Saracens', brought it to France in 1260 when returning from the Crusades. It has masses of crimson flowers gilded with golden stamens and a delectable scent. Then there is its sport *R. gallica* 'Versicolor', Rosa Mundi, Fair Rosamund's rose, with all the same delights as its parent, and almost as ancient. There are two Damask roses, 'Kazanlik' (*R. × damascena* 'Trigintipetala'), grown in Bulgaria to make attar of roses, and York and Lancaster (*R. × damascena* var. *versicolor*). This last, legend tells us, was the rose from which, during the Wars of the Roses, each side took a flower, one red, one white. On the walls of the palace, I planted *R. moschata*, the musk rose, very ancient and probably in England since the time of Elizabeth I. Its delicious scent pervades the air from August to the autumn.

So much for the roses, which are planted in a *mélange* with other ancient plants, prominent amongst them the martagon lilies, a dusky pink growing abundantly with their white brothers. They are not only in the beds where I planted them but have seeded in the banks around the garden, as have the primroses and cowslips, and masses of ladies' bedstraw has appeared with its delicious scent of new-mown hay. I planted these banks with *Fritillaria meleagris*, Gerard's 'chequered daffodil'. They flower in May, and with them *Muscari botryoides* 'Album', which came from Spain and could have been brought from there by Tradescant. It has a sweet scent, likened by Parkinson to 'starch when it is made new and hot'.

When these banks are in full bloom with fritillaries, white grape hyacinths, cowslips and primroses, thick with their flowers, for all the world they look like the flowering meadow of Botticelli's *Primavera*.

I had quite forgot to speak of the crown imperials I planted in the knots. There are only two varieties, a red one and a yellow one, and they have never changed since their arrival from Persia and Turkey and their introduction to Europe by Clusius, who collected plants for the Emperor. If you turn up the flower, you will see teardrops within. They are perpetual, and nothing, neither shaking nor breaking, will dislodge them. It is said that it will for ever hold its tears, tears of shame, for failing to bow its head when Our Lord passed by.

After many years had gone by, the fountain from Italy became sadly decayed and had to be removed. There were other priorities and so the Knot Garden was disgraced by a drab-looking fountainless pool until 2001. At that time I was reading the *Hypnerotomachia Poliphili*, and one of the drawings showing a boy standing on a sphere and blowing a trumpet struck me as being the perfect figure for the Knot Garden

fountain. It had not only been drawn in the 1490s, very close to the date when the Old Palace was built, but had been designed for a garden. There was an exact description of how it was made. The boy had a hole in the back of his head and a wing below him. The wind caught the wing, which turned the figure, and then the wind entered the hole in his head and blew the trumpet. There was no description of the sort of sound it made, but one supposes it might have sounded somewhat like an Aeolian harp. What a challenge to create a fountain figure from a drawing and description over five hundred years old!

I decided to take up the challenge and got in touch with the expert and resourceful Mr Franklin, who had worked as organizer and manager of the works carried out at Hatfield by the Cambridge firm Rattee and Kett over thirty years or more. He gallantly came out of retirement to help, joining Mr Beaumont with his practical knowledge of almost every craft, Mr Tony Darwin, mason and man of many other skills, plus his mate Mr Alvin Shelsher, and Mr Wilson who fashioned reeds for the trumpet. Within something over a year, the octagon-shaped limestone fountain, made in China, was in place and the golden boy, complete with trumpet and wing, now reigns in gilded glory over the palace garden. The sound from his trumpet is as yet only a faint whisper, but that is being worked on, and what they achieved in 1492 surely can be accomplished with all the new technology of the twenty-first century.

My time at Hatfield has now drawn to a close. My swan song has been sung – and I hope that the vision and dream I had over thirty years ago, when I first came to Hatfield, that one day the gardens there would become as harmonious as a woman's face in the right hat, may have been, at least partially, fulfilled. That it is a place that approaches a little nearer to being my ideal garden: one planted with deliciously fragrant homely plants like those that filled the gardens of the Tudors and Stuarts with sweetness and the hum of bees, and also a place of fancies and conceits, which would, together, fulfil the idea of a garden as a place where pleasure and peace are both to be found.

Then I could exclaim, as did St Bernard, 'Good God, what a company of pleasures thou hast made for man!'

Above The Knot Garden, its bright intricate box threads enclosing plants from medieval, Tudor and Jacobean times
Opposite Plan for the Knot Garden

HELMINGHAM HALL

SUFFOLK

Lord and Lady Tollemache

Opposite Helmingham Hall
from the north
Below Looking over the knot
garden back to the Hall

As you emerge from a double avenue of ancient oaks, your eye is immediately engaged by the sight of a house with an air of romance and picturesque beauty, surrounded by a moat with a drawbridge that is still drawn up every night. The park of this Tudor courtyard house, its rosy-red brick deliciously enhanced by the greens of grass and tree, is grazed by the descendants of the fallow and red deer that roamed it for many centuries. The beauty of the distant views enchants the eye as you leave the shadows of the great oaks and emerge into the sunlight.

The same family has lived in this Tudor hall since 1510, except for a period of forty years, a Tollemache having married the heiress of Helmingham, and the family have lived in Suffolk from shortly after the Norman Conquest. The member of the family who lived here before the present Lord Tollemache's parents was an Aunt May, who occupied only a few rooms and took to staying under an umbrella in the house because the roof leaked – or was it, Lady Tollemache asks, just an eccentricity?

The 1st Lord Tollemache built a castle in Cheshire and lived at Helmingham for only half the year. From two wives he had twenty-four sons and a daughter, and to accommodate them he enlarged the Tudor rooms at Helmingham, which has been a boon to his descendants today, who need the space for entertaining and for functions.

It is my first visit to Helmingham, and I have come at the behest of the Tollemaches, Lady Tollemache having asked if I would design a garden for her. Lord Tollemache thinks that work on the gardens was started some years after his family moved to Helmingham in the early sixteenth century. Old maps and drawings show that the original shape of the main walled garden predates the house by many years; it was most probably of Saxon origin and constructed to protect stock from marauders. There was a wooded palisade to protect the garden from deer until the present garden wall was built in 1745.

There can be little doubt that in those early years the gardens around the house would have been typical of their time: a garden of simples – herbs for medicine, for the kitchen and for strewing on the floors – with the few flowers and bulbs there were available for making tussie-mussies and nosegays, occasionally carried in an effort to combat the unpleasant smells only too commonly around. The exotic flowers from the New World and those from Constantinople and Persia had not yet arrived to excite and astonish the botanists and gardeners of Europe.

Lady Tollemache wanted a garden to harmonize historically and aesthetically with the Tudor house and knew that I had been designing and making knot gardens for the fifteenth-century palace at Hatfield (see pages 81–87), which was almost exactly the same date as Helmingham. She wished to incorporate a herb garden, and a garden of old-fashioned roses (she had acquired a passion for these from that great lover of the old roses, Humphrey Brooke). Another part of the design was to create, in box, the family fret, a heraldic device which Lady Tollemache had discovered carved in wood over a mantelpiece. Some of the box hedges were to be clipped like interlacing ribbons in the correct manner of early knot gardens. The whole garden was to be surrounded by high yew hedges.

It could not have been a happier commission, just my period, and I could not have had a more delightful client. With a great love of plants and gardens, Lady Tollemache was at the start of a glittering career as a garden designer and was to go on to win two gold medals at the Chelsea Flower Show. I am rather glad I could not look into the future at that moment, as I might not have dared to take on the job.

Here is my 'plan for a new garden at Helmingham', sent to Lady Tollemache in February 1981.

'I feel this garden should be a visual and architectural extension of the house. Ideally it should be of the utmost simplicity because if it is to be in happy harmony with the house, it should strive to be what it most surely would have been if it had been created at the time the house was built, although we must not be too purist about this but must be ready to accept what would have certainly taken place over the next two hundred years. Embellishments there surely must have been in this time as well as more fundamental alterations, but they would all have been architecturally and visually related to the architecture of the house in 1700. Only later did the rot set in with the decadence of the eighteenth-century gardens and the landscape school.

'Of course there may never have been a formal garden in this place, though looking at the ground and surveying the raised walk which, like mounts, were built "to be clambered up to view a fair prospect", the fair prospect always being a fair garden, formal and well ordered, I feel that there is a strong probability there was a garden here.

'I said ideally the garden should be of the utmost simplicity, firstly for the foregoing reason, but there is a second reason and a most important one which in 1982 really is essential. It has to be capable of

Opposite and above Three views of the garden I designed for Helmingham in 1981. A broad path leading to a statue forms the main axis of the garden, which terminates in an archway formed in the solid yew hedge that surrounds the knots and beds filled with pastel-toned flowers, herbs and old-fashioned roses. There are knots both in bold geometric shapes and in more intricate interlaced designs clipped so that the box strands appear woven.

being maintained by the least possible labour. Fortunately, achieving the first should achieve the second.

'Before I set out the ideal plantings for such a garden, I would like to say that we must not set out to slavishly copy a garden of the fifteenth century, but what we should try and achieve is a garden which has strongly the manner and feeling of the time of the house, or it will never be in a happy harmony with it and visually satisfying to the heart and eye.

'This does not mean that you can never plant plants and bulbs introduced after 1700 – but I think it does mean that "modern" colour, many modern hybrids and Hybrid Teas and Floribundas should be avoided like the plague along with a modern style of placing plants in blocks and groupings. A slightly cottagey effect should be aimed for. At that time, plants were chiefly for use in the house for cooking and in medicine so the gardens were planted practically as well as for pleasure. Herbs were planted liberally of course – as well as carnations, pinks, roses, lilies and the new tulips.

'There is a very large choice of plants to be made and it is an error to think you will be overly restricted in the variety of plants and bulbs suitable for a period garden, and that will look suitable and happy there. There are many delightful almost forgotten plants that would, I'm sure, be a great joy to grow again that have, owing to the takeover of novelties and new hybrids especially in the last fifty years, become lost and forgotten pleasures.'

Lady Tollemache accepted these suggestions and the work was put in hand.

It is now twenty-five years since I designed that garden for Helmingham and although I had seen photographs of it, I went back to see it only in May 2006. I had by then almost forgotten what I had designed so many years ago. You could liken the situation to having your tiny baby adopted, only to discover, twenty-five years later, that your baby had turned into a beautiful young man.

Left, above White foxgloves, lavender and a mound of old roses
Left, below An oriental poppy
Right One of the many old-fashioned roses at Helmingham

HIGHGROVE

GLOUCESTERSHIRE

HRH The Prince of Wales

Many accounts have been written of the gardens at Highgrove, the home of His Royal Highness The Prince of Wales. However, as I was involved in the birth of the garden, I thought that I might be able to dredge up from my memories – some of which are clear and vivid – and with the help of innumerable letters, bills, papers and some sketches and plans, a few, so far unrecorded descriptions of its creation. This was all of twenty-six years ago.

My first view of Highgrove was from the back of a horse (which I believe was His Royal Highness's first view of it too). The hounds were in full cry after a fox found in a cover near Badminton. It was heading for an ancient ivy-covered oak tree in a large paddock at Highgrove, where it often lay up, and this was far from the first time it had led the pack to its sanctuary. As I leapt the post and rails surrounding the paddock, the house came into view.

The Prince had seen the gardens at Cranborne and Hatfield and also the garden I had designed for my cousin (see page 42). He must have liked what he saw for he asked me if I would work on designing the gardens at Highgrove. The first person he had invited to do the garden was my friend Lanning Roper, who with his long experience, great knowledge and perfect taste would have done a wonderful job, but his health was failing and he could not take it on. The Prince was eager to get started immediately and I made an exhaustive tour of the grounds. There were some good trees, including the now well-known ancient cedar of Lebanon on the west side of the house. Otherwise there was little planting of interest – no gardens, just a few beds immediately under the house walls. And there were no hedges. The land was flat and featureless, with the house exposed and unprotected on at least three sides, especially to the east where the spire of Tetbury church could be seen – an attractive feature, but it emphasised the immediate need for a good screen, or screens, to protect from cameras and prying eyes, which could only too easily come from the direction of the little market town of Tetbury.

The Prince came on visits to Cranborne to discuss the garden, and plans were spread out on the drawing room floor to be pored over, adapted or adopted. I felt the very first thing to do was to lay out the skeleton, the frame of the garden: the terraces, south and west with their hedges or whatever plantings or materials enclosed them; the yew hedges that defined the different spaces; and the paths that led you to them. So this the Prince and I set out to do.

The soil was alkaline, not aggressively so, but it would not be possible to grow rhododendrons or azaleas, which was a disappointment for the Prince, though I am afraid I was rather pleased. They are beautiful plants, particularly the species and the scented ones, and they look well in places like Cornwall and the west of Scotland, but they seem to me somewhat alien in a garden where they cannot thrive without much help.

Some way from the house there was a large brick-walled kitchen garden, with a small orchard of fruit trees and an old circular pond which had been filled in, but little else. When I first saw it, it was a sea of mud, but it was a very promising space and it was here that the Prince wanted me to design a garden for flowers, vegetables and fruit, on the lines of the one I had designed and planted in the west country My architect friend made a scale plan for me and I set to work to do the design.

Above The cedar of Lebanon, from the flower garden
Opposite The south façade of Highgrove. A mown grass path leads through the wildflower meadow.

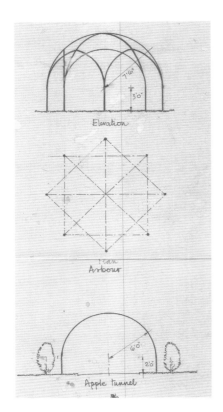

Above Sketches for the metalwork for the apple tunnel and – in plan and in perspective – the domed arbours

The garden was to have four large squares with slender paths giving access to the beds within the squares. Each square had a different pattern of beds, and all was outlined with box hedging. Tunnels were constructed with curving metal arches rising from low apple hedges. The arches would have apples trained over them, and the narrow beds on either side of the central path were to be planted with hellebores and polyanthus, both happy in the half-shade. These apple tunnels, running from both sides of the garden, east to west, led into a large area outlined by a circle of standard *Malus* 'Golden Hornet', their linked branches creating in the spring a circle of blossom and in the autumn a golden crown of fruit. In the centre of the circle was the old pond, and here I felt there should be a fountain, but a simple one, no fancy figures or jets. I found what I believed to be just the thing in Italy, and, with the Prince's approval, it was ordered. It had a plain central bowl on a pedestal with a smaller bowl above and the water bubbled up to flow down into the basin, making a restful and satisfying sound. Here, I felt, unshaded and in full sun, was the perfect place for a garden of herbs. A double row of curved beds, edged in brick and with narrow paths dividing them, was laid around the fountain, and I planted the back beds entirely with rosemary and the front ones with a herb collection that the Women's Institute had given to the Prince and Princess as a wedding present.

The kitchen garden was a quiet haven away from the bustling life that went on in less protected places in the garden. The two young princes were tiny boys then – in fact when I started to design the garden, there was only one. Prince Charles had a low white-painted picket fence made to surround the fountain so that it was safe for them.

Left Potatoes and fruit trees
in the walled kitchen garden
Opposite The apple tunnel in
the kitchen garden

The paths in the four squares led into circular domed arbours and I have just found the list of the plants I put there to cover them, chosen so that two arbours would be in flower at the same time and all four would have something in flower. There were roses 'Seagull', 'Climbing Pompon de Paris', 'Albertine', 'Emily Gray' and 'Adelaide d'Orleans', 'Sander's White', *Clematis montana* and three wisterias, *W. sinensis*, *W.s.* 'Pink Ice' and *W. floribunda* 'Snow Showers'. The Prince had chairs put in each of the arbours, though it was seldom he sat on them, more likely he would, secateurs in hand, be pruning something.

The garden had a broad central walk running from north to south. Here wide borders were made and planted with roses and many of the Prince's favourite herbaceous plants. I remember ordering for him some dark purple delphiniums, which he especially liked, but there were herbaceous peonies too, sage and grey-foliaged plants. Dennis Brown was the star of the show, for it was he who grew the vegetables, and magnificent they were. There is nothing, to my mind, more beautiful than an orderly kitchen garden and Dennis was the man to create it. With the vegetables he grew in his own garden he had won every local prize that was going, and now the Prince was lucky enough to have Dennis growing his. I first remember Dennis in his green hunt coat whipping in the hounds on hunting days with the Beaufort, and keeping them in the just as good order as he does his vegetables.

One of the very first things I wanted to do was to give the Prince some protection near the house where he would be sheltered not only from prying eyes, but from the east and west winds. The southern side of the house was chosen and the immediate job was to plant a protective wall of yew, which would enclose a garden on three sides. The Prince was pessimistic about how long the yew hedges would take to grow but I persuaded him that if his yews were planted at 2.5-3 feet high in a deep trench with broken-up chalk at the bottom, a layer of well-rotted farmyard manure and a final layer of top soil, then mulched with the same farmyard manure each autumn, and not allowed to dry out in the summer (which might entail, in especially hot weather, spraying the foliage in the evening or early morning when the sun was not on it), the hedge should, and would grow 12 to 18 inches a year. So to be able to have hedges 6 feet high in three years was not a fantasy.

The first thing to do once the yew was planted was to make a paved terrace, while widening the borders under the house. Here the Prince wanted a garden filled with old-fashioned roses and scented plants, pinks, violas, lilies and lavender, somewhere where he could sit and enjoy the sights and scents. This was not difficult to achieve and I got him a round limestone table from Italy which he could work on, and in the paving either side made a pair of beds which I planted with grey scented plants.

While these planting plans presented no problems, the proportions of the garden did. It was important that they should look right in relation to the height of the house. There were various underground

When well planted and well cared for, yew is relatively fast-growing. It forms an impressive protective boundary around the south garden at Highgrove.

fittings that had to be put in place, and I was dismayed to learn that these would restrict the length of the garden too severely for it to look right. However, a compromise was reached and although I would have liked to be able to make it longer, I think the proportions just get away with it.

I had, of course, always hoped that the Prince would garden organically, as I had done since 1948. I I introduced the Prince to HDRA, and soon afterwards he became their Patron. I also introduced him to a great friend of mine, Miriam Rothschild, the famous scientist and expert on fleas, worms, butterflies and wild flowers (and countless other things).

The Prince wanted to have wild flowers in the meadow areas around the house and Miriam suggested making a butterfly garden. I designed this in a place on the way to the swimming pool, and Miriam gave me the names of the plants that that most attracted butterflies. The garden was soon completed. Then, following Miriam's advice – and after the careful preparation she stipulated – we sowed in the grass bordering the entrance drive the seed of the famous 'farmers' nightmare', as she had christened it: a mixture of corn marigolds, poppies, ox-eye daisies, cornflowers and corn cockles. For a time it was a losing battle with the grass, which was too long and lush, even though we also sowed yellow rattle, a parasite on

The meadows around the house were sown with butterfly-attracting wild flowers.

A springtime view of he enclosed garden on the south of the house, with beds planted with black and white flowers

grass roots, in a bid to thin it. Eventually, however, some of the wild flowers became established.

I drew a plan for the west terrace garden with low walls outlining it and an octagonal pool in its centre. The Prince was keen to have a pergola that would lead from the right of this terrace to the swimming pool. The pool was a gift, as was the stone paving that surrounded it, and he liked the idea of encircling it with a sweetbrier hedge. We planted this. Then, over a metal crossed arch above the gate leading from the pool westwards, I trained a pair of 'Golden Hornet' crab apples, their blossom a scented mass of pink and white, and their fruit a golden bow.

This gate led into an area with a lot of shrubs, bushes and small trees, with a certain number of mature trees. Much clearing had to be done here and some new planting of more choice varieties of trees and shrubs. We also made a mown grass path to traverse this area, curving in one place round a specimen tree encircled by a wooden seat. The path takes you out into the open where as you have to your left the west façade of the house, you look over a raised rectangular pond. This was a problem because it seemed out of scale and detached from any coherent plan. The large lumps of golden yews lining the sides of the path leading to the house presented another difficulty. I was marginally in favour of getting rid of them, golden yews not being great favourites of mine, but the Prince was reluctant to take them out and they have now been topiaried, each one in different bizarre ways, and have taken on a character of their own.

There was one thing that took up a great deal of my time and that was dealing with the presents that were given to the Prince and Princess for the gardens. I have already mentioned the herb collection presented by the Women's Institute. In addition, the Fruiterers' Company gave the fruit for the kitchen garden, the Royal Horticultural Society

said they would like to give a generous number of plants, and there were many individual gifts of trees and plants. Some of the donors wanted to come and see where their gifts were to be planted. One group of ladies said they would like to come and plant their gift themselves, and nearly all the donors wanted a list naming the trees or plants the Prince would like to have, and, of course, quite rightly, so they could source the best specimens, they all wanted the information at once. It was not easy to reply as the garden and its planning was far from completed and much thought had still be given to what would go where.

I met Mr Todd of the Fruiterers' Company because it was necessary for him to see where the fruit they had given was to be planted in the kitchen garden: the site for the proposed apple hedges and apple-covered arches forming the tunnels, for instance, as well as the aspects of the walks surrounding the garden and the walls facing north where morello cherries would be planted. Mr Todd wanted a list of fruit the Prince might like to have. I sent him this and, reading my accompanying letter, I see I mentioned he would especially like some of the fruit that was particularly delicious but had passed out of fashion because it was not commercially viable.

Various cities gave gifts. Lists of roses arrived, a birdbath was offered. A sundial, a gift of the staff at Badminton, was placed in the centre of the south terrace garden. All were accompanied or preceded by letters, and a complex correspondence was built up between many participants – the donors, the Prince's offices in Buckingham Palace, the Duchy of Cornwall, myself, sometimes the Prince himself – and it fell to me to meet some of the donors and to place their gifts.

Interesting as this task was, and I met some splendid people in the doing of it, it was a relief when it was finished and I could concentrate on the rest of the job. There were many bulbs to be planted, apart from those we put in the beds around the house and in the terrace gardens. There were wild areas to be planted with snowdrops, narcissus, bluebells, anemones and martagon lilies, which don't mind a bit of alkaline and could happily seed about in the grass, as would cowslips. Primroses, and oxlips as well, could go in the woodland.

I suggested a low tapestry hedge to run along the outside of the plantation and the wood to the south-east of the house, which was made up almost entirely of larch, but which was to become an arboretum.

The enclosed garden in mid-summer, the central sundial surrounded by exuberant planting contained in neatly box-edged beds with topiary corners

Above One of the topiaried gateways in the garden
Opposite The gazebo – one of a pair – in the courtyard garden on the west side of the house

The tapestry hedge would be planted with hornbeam and holly, beech, possibly some box, and evergreen oak – such a hedge is a most decorative thing, and separates well the more sophisticated areas of the garden from the wilder parts. A roughly mown grass path would run along its north side, and some particularly decorative specimen trees, a few of them flowering ones, and others chosen for the beauty of their leaves or autumn colouring, were planted here and there on the other side of the path, allowing sun to penetrate and agreeable glimpses of the house and flowering meadows to be seen.

I think that was about all the work I did for the Prince of Wales, apart from searching for the perfect head gardener for him, which again entailed much correspondence. I also found an architect to build the dovecote he had always wanted to have at Highgrove. David Blisset, who had done some work for me on other projects, designed it. It is built in the local stone, with stone tiles on the roof, and sits in perfect harmony with the landscape around the house. It was in just such a happy harmony that my days were spent working and designing for the Prince at Highgrove all those years ago.

CHATEAU DE ST CLOU

PROVENCE

The Marquess and Marchioness of Salisbury

A view over the Petit Jardin to the farmhouse and the towers of the château

'I think we might buy a house abroad.' I was stunned by this announcement. It came from my husband of forty-five years, who had clearly been turning the idea over in his mind for some considerable time. 'Don't you think your family have enough houses already?' I cautiously replied, while feeling a mounting

excitement as before my eyes flashed a certainly unreal vision of a delectable house in Italy or France, bathed in everlasting sunshine, wreathed in vines, roses and jasmine, its garden smelling of lavender, basil and rosemary . . . Come down to earth, I said to myself, and let's talk practicalities. Where shall this house be? Old age was advancing and we would have ideally liked to be able to spend a week, or even a long weekend, in the place, so Italy seemed to be too far off, though the thought of its delights and our many friends there made it hard to abandon. Spain, we knew only a little, though liking what we knew, but again like Italy, distances for elderly folk were a crab. So France, it seemed, was the country to choose, and we settled down to think of the best and most practical area to explore for a house.

The number one need was warmth for the greatest part of the year, so that eliminated a large part of France. The southern coast was unconsidered as well; largely wrecked by development, it held no appeal for us. It would be helpful not to be too far from an airport, and a piece of unspoilt country away from tourists and English settlers. Were we asking for the moon?

We would see. Provence sounded a part of the country that might hold what we sought, so one day, with a couple of weeks to spare, we climbed into the car, hovercrafted across the Channel and headed for Provence, which we quartered, noting the parts we liked the best. Back in England, I rang an old friend of my Irish uncle and aunt, who lived in Provence, to ask her advice. 'Come and stay,' she said at once, and so we did. She put us in touch with a local agent and gave us much sound advice. A packet full of photographs and descriptions of houses arrived for us as the result of contact with the agent, and after weeding out the rogues, we drove to visit those we felt were possibilities. Some of these we did not even get out of the car to look at further; a glance at the house, or the country around, or both, was enough for us to realize they would not do.

There was one delightful property, with an enclosed courtyard entered under an archway with a gatehouse above it. The house, gatehouse, and courtyard walls were all built in the local limestone, probably around the late eighteenth century, and it had a narrow balcony running round its middle with a very simple but pretty wrought-iron railing, from which you could have contemplated a courtyard garden.

It was only with reluctance we decided against exploring it further, and our reasons for deciding this were that the house was situated in an area known as *garrigue*, which is rocky terrain with few trees, except for smallish evergreen oaks. The scent as you walk in the *garrigue* is delicious and all pervading, of plants such as thyme, rosemary and lavender, not billowing or luxuriating but small and tough, surviving in the harsh terrain, parched by the summer heat, touched by frost in winter, tenaciously clinging to life in the stones and sparse earth, their roots seeking rare moisture and food beneath the rocks. The *garrigue* had great attraction, but the fact that it has few large trees was a sign that water was sparse, although there had, we noticed, been a well in the courtyard of the house. My husband had said he would not consider a house that did not have a spring, and I felt that the choice of the kind of garden that could be created there would be limited by the terrain, and of the plants that would happily grow within it there would surely be an even lesser choice. So we said goodbye to it, and after looks at one or two others, returned home, hoping the agent would soon produce a few more for us to see.

One day we had a call from our friend who had so kindly had us to stay. 'I've found it, I've found it!' she cried. 'You must come at once. It has a stone terrace with stone lions on it, a *pigeonnier*, a *chapelle* and a farm in the valley below.' Collecting as many of the family as possible, we bundled into an aeroplane and were met at the airport by our friend, who drove us, at breakneck speed, in her open car to this 'dream' house, her enthusiasm overriding meaner thoughts that invaded our minds such as, It sounds a rather dauntingly considerable place. The drive, through woods of huge trees (so there was water), swept uphill and arrived at the house. All that our friend had described was there – the stone lions, terraces, a *chapelle*, the *pigeonnier*, the small ancient farm, which could be glimpsed in the valley below – but the château was enormous, having fifty-six rooms. Sadly we drove away without seeing the inside, which was perhaps rather unenterprising, but there might have been a temptation, though this thought was not in our minds at that moment. We were perhaps too disappointed to want to see any more.

'There is another house for sale, not far from here,' said our friend, as we drove in silence. 'Would you like to look at it?' We agreed that we would, and after a short drive arrived at a dilapidated château sitting in dilapidated surroundings, with an air of being unloved and uncared for. It had not been listed amongst the ones given to us by our agent, but our friend had heard by chance that it was for sale.

It had been bought by a property developer who found small farmhouses in Provence, did them up and then sold them on at a profit. Apparently, he had had his eye on this place for some time, finally managing to buy it from its then owner, M. Manon, whose wife had recently died, leaving him with an only child, a daughter. M. Manon had been left the property by his godmother, an *antiquaire*, who had bought it around 1900. She had apparently been staying in the area and, needing some chickens, had heard that there were excellent fowl to be found at the Château de St Clou. Ordering her carriage, she drove over to the château, fell in love with it and bought both it and the chickens. Her godson was a soldier, whose home was at Lyon. He was not at all interested in Provençal life, which largely revolves around grape growing and wine making and the tending of olive groves and orchards of cherries and apricots. However, when his godmother died, leaving him the property, he gave up his army life and came down to live at St Clou. He had sold it to the property developer only five years before we first saw it, and during that time the man had managed to carry out a great deal of destructive work on the château and its immediate surroundings. For all its sad state, we felt an immediate attraction to the place.

There were many large trees, predominantly oaks, of great height, sporting trunks that spoke of long years of growth, as well as umbrella pines and a large number of plane trees, some forming a fine avenue on the northern side of the château. The *pré*, or meadow, there led to a bank crowned by oaks, planes and cypress with *Viburnum tinus*, yews, wild clematis and many other wild flowers, or the remains of them, scattered through the fringe of open woodland bordering a river. The river flowed over a high cascade falling into a pool below, in which were a few trout, lazily swishing their tails.

On the east side of the château there was an enclosed garden surrounded by a low wall topped by stone slabs which you could see had once had iron railings mounted on them. Indeed, later we found these in a *remise* or barn, and I did not regret that they had been removed, for they were not pretty, nineteenth century and painted a pale apple green. At the east end of this enclosed garden were the ruins of what must have been a twelve- to fourteen-foot-high structure, at the foot of which was a large stone trough for water with above it, set in the stone, a sculptured stone dolphin. Part of its tail was missing, but luckily there was enough left of the tail for a visiting Italian archaeologist, an expert on Roman remains, to identify it as a Roman dolphin. The garden was a dump of earth, stones and weeds, quite overgrown with five yew trees which must have been thirty or forty years old, as well as an immensely tall, and gracefully branched, *Gleditsia triacanthos*, centred on the east entrance to the château. The main door was on its southern side, with a plantation of mature trees to the east, including

A view of the château from
the north, with the avenue of
planes (*Platanus* x *hispanica*)
marking the entrance drive

a tall Scots pine, three fine planes and five or six yews, a couple of which must have been at least two
hundred years old and another perhaps even older. Either side of the drive there was a planting of horse
chestnuts, forming a short avenue, and also a lime tree.

A view of the château from the north, with the avenue of planes (*Platanus* x *hispanica*) marking the entrance drive

Attached to the château to the west was a farmhouse. While the main house appeared to be around
mid-eighteenth century, this building looked a century earlier. There was a large stone basin in front of
it with a sloping place in its rim for scrubbing and washing clothes, and a deep and gracefully shaped
half-moon bowl at its northern end, backed by a carved stone, which clearly had had some kind of
decorative piece at its top. Water flowed from a metal pipe into the bowl. The basin must have been
not only for washing clothes but also for watering animals and filling water pots. There was an overflow
from a stone pipe, so there was certainly a spring – another plus for the place. We were gathering more
and more pluses as we poked around.

The living rooms of the farmhouse were joined to the château by three huge *remises* divided by three-
foot-thick stone walls, their arched entrances filled by wooden doors, though some of these were

missing altogether, and all were bashed and broken, with only traces of paint. Above the *remises* were three arched-topped windows, unglazed – *granges* or granaries, evidently, for animal feeding stuffs. Then came the farmhouse itself, with its entrance door, an immense oak affair with iron studs and dropping handle. Inside was the farmhouse kitchen with a Louis XIII chimneypiece in stone and above was a well-planned apartment created by the present owner.

On the west side of the farmhouse there were the remains of some small buildings recently pulled down, probably pigsties or goat pens. The land beyond was in parts level, in parts sloping down across the meadows to the trees and the river below. On the south-west of the entrance drive lay, between the narrow public road and the château, a vineyard. The château itself looked to be in a pretty parlous state, its walls bare of plaster in many places, revealing the randomly sized stones with which it was built. No one seemed to know its exact age, but it was probably built in the mid-eighteenth century, about 1767, as a country house or shooting lodge, the kind of château known in Provence as a *bastide*.

It had a curiously attractive exterior. It was basically square and at each corner there was a tower, which was round on the outer side and flat on the inner. These towers rose some six feet higher than the roof with robust stone parapets supported by corbels. In an earlier era, when defence had to be thought of, this parapet would have had openings between the supporting corbels for dropping stones or boiling lead on assailants.

The château's south, east and north façades (the west façade had the farmhouse, sheds and barns attached to it) lacked some windows: some were blocked up, largely to the north, against, we were told later, the blows of the fierce mistral that blew, chiefly after rain had fallen and especially savagely in February. Starting in Germany, this famous wind hits the Massive Central and turns down the Rhône to blow in Provence and the Mediterranean provinces of France on odd days – one, three, five, seven and so on. Like all persistent winds, it can become extremely irritating: doors and windows rattle and bang, branches crash down, the gardens are littered with leaves and detritus and you are driven into the house, however warm and sunny it may be, by the impossibility of reading your newspapers or book in tranquillity. After some days of suffering, it is easier to understand why, if evidence is produced during a murder trial that a mistral has been blowing at the time of the crime, it is still considered a mitigating circumstance.

Having tripped up over two Roman busts, a man and a woman, not so speak of noticing a pair of stone pineapples in what looked like the tops of gate piers hidden beneath mountains of weed-covered earth and stones, we began to feel that there was something rather appealing about this place.

Now came the moment to go into the house. The entrance hall's floor was laid with reddish nineteenth-century tiles, decorated and rather shiny, not pretty, but the staircase was a gem: the first flight was stone, the banisters oak and carved flat in a simple shape, and it swept, in a rather grand way, up to the first floor. What happened beyond we couldn't see, but later we were to discover it was the same the whole way to the top floor, except the treads changed from stone to tiles.

The salon was a sad sight. The chimneypiece had been ripped out, leaving a gaping hole, which had largely destroyed and made irreparable the decorative plasterwork, known in Provence as *gypseries*. The walls had been hung with a dark-flowered cotton which hung in rags to the floor, set, like the hall, with red shiny tiles. The petit salon next door was dark and almost windowless. The north entrance room was divided by a thin wooden partition, the smallest part forming a primitive kitchen with a shallow stone sink and one cold tap – which appeared to be the only source of water in the château. On the

The stone *bassin*, used in the past for watering farm animals and washing clothes, on the south of the château

other side of the partition was the north entrance door and on its side jutting into the room was an enormous ironbound wooden barrel. Any windows there were seemed to be blocked up. A narrow doorway led into a small room occupying the first floor of the north-east tower. A hole in the floor had steep stone steps leading down into an exceedingly damp cellar, where another immense barrel lay.

We had not discovered one bath, loo or basin and decided that there were not any. Finally, we completed our rough survey of the place with a stumbling inspection of what, on the château's northern face, must have originally been a terrace with a perron or stairway leading to the *prés* or meadows down below but now had only a rough wooden platform jutting out, supposedly of use when the grapes were brought in from the vineyards in early autumn.

Well, what did we think of it? What was the verdict?

To go for it. It might seem quite dotty to think this, as we stood inside the mouldering rooms and contemplated the near ruins of the outside. But 'It has a nice atmosphere,' we both said. In 1986, we bought the château and a small amount of land around it, and the restoration began.

The château had belonged to the de Sade family, and was one of their several properties in the Vaucluse. Lacoste was the principal one, and the château lived in by the author of the infamous book, lately reprinted after many years of repression. The de Sade who lived in St Clou was an *évêque*, or bishop, uncle to the wicked Marquis, and legend has it that when the authorities were in full cry after the Marquis and seeking to arrest him and take him to the Bastille, he fled Lacoste and took refuge with his uncle at St Clou, who is believed to have been almost as wicked as his nephew. Whether or not they caught up with the Marquis and arrested him in the château is a matter of speculation. While our repairs to the château were in full swing, the then Marquis turned up, saying he much wanted to buy his old family property, and was it thought that we might consider selling it. The answer was that it was unlikely.

After the de Sades, it was bought by the Marquis d'Isinard, from a Vauclusian family, who owned anther property, with a fine château, near the town of Carpentras. The next owner was the *antiquaire* who bought it and the chickens. It was perhaps rather unusual for three marquises to have owned the place.

I had, of course, from the first sight of St Clou, been contemplating and summing up the possibilities of creating a garden there. I had read the book *Perfume from Provence* by Winifred Fortescue and one or two other volumes which described gardening in the south, but I did not do enough research, which was idiotic, as there was a great deal to learn of which I was quite ignorant, such as how low the temperature could fall in the winter, was there much snow and did it lie for long, what was the average rainfall in the year and other information of the kind which would be necessary if I were to be able to garden successfully. My foolish head had equated Provence with a climate that warmed old bones, more or less perpetual sun, a garden which would grow near semi-tropical plants and an air balmy and laden with the scents of lavender and tender jasmines, not to speak of walls hung with tea roses.

Thank God we came in February to supervise the building operations, and by a great bit of luck we hit on a mistral, which was blowing as only a mistral can (we were to learn later) in February. Several inches of snow also fell before we left, which was a mercy as we had, with our heads full of the idea of pretty well twelve months of delicious warmth and surely mild winters, told the architect we would not want central heating. With frozen fingers, I dialled his number, anxiously wondering if it would, with several operations in the château already completed, be now too late to install it. Mercifully all was well and it could be done, but there was a nervous moment or two before we had his answer.

In the olive walk, with Bonnie

There was now so much going on in and about the house that to begin to think how a garden might be shaped around it was not practical. Wheelbarrows, cement mixers, piles of sand, stones and rubbish from the house littered the ground; weeds were thigh high, growing on mounds in the walled garden. I tripped over a lump of stone in one such heap and discovered a Roman bust – I tried to lift it, but it was too heavy and next time I was there it had gone. It was not a bad thing to have this time before making plans for the garden, as I could begin to get a feel of the place, assess the spaces around the château, distances and proportions, look out from the house on each of the three floors through often windowless stone frames and absorb the views.

To the east, you looked towards the dramatic Mont Ventoux, at 1,900 metres (6,233 feet) the highest mountain in the south of France, its top snow-covered in winter, its slopes enjoyed by skiers. When the snows melted in May, it was hard to tell when they were gone, as beneath them lay a covering of chalk stones, an immense field of astonishing whiteness. There were patterns of light and darkness, the clouds, sometimes snowy white and billowing against a smooth blue sky, at other times purple and black with a look of menace, threatening a savage storm. At dawn the reds and gold of the rising sun changed from the deepest red to the palest rose, by which time you'd rushed to a south window to watch it spreading slowly from the east to wash with pink the southern sky.

From the north-facing windows on the top floor, you looked down from a considerable height to the *prés*, which stretched down to the trees bordering the river. Above and beyond the trees rose Les Dentelles de Montmirail, their 'lace' a crown of limestone mountains eroded by the wind to form an ever-changing pattern, a fantasy of lace-like pillars and arches. When the light was clear and bright, as when rain was coming, they seemed near; in the burning heat of summer they retreated to become a mere backcloth; when the sun was setting in the western skies, its reflection on the columns and peaks of Montmirral's lace made them look as if painted in gold leaf.

This protracted looking about the place, from the inside out and outside in, was no bad thing to have done. Looking back, I believe it helped me to absorb and feel the spirit and character of the land and the house that stood within it. To be able to note the horizontals and the perpendiculars, the highs and the lows, the changing light in the different seasons and the colours with their dramatic variations in almost every month helped me begin to understand what might be needed to achieve a harmony of design between the garden and the house– not forgetting what would be seen outside the garden, the terrain that was uncultivated, with its indigenous trees, shrubs and wild flowers.

Clearing the rubbish was the first task and I began on the walled garden on the east side of the château. When the clearance was finished, five large old yew trees and a horse chestnut had gone and a fountain had been revealed – not a pretty one, alas! But there was at least water in the centre of the garden, and even a tiny brass tap which, when the pipe had been unblocked, worked a simple jet. The water came from a spring, which encouraged us to think that it might be possible to irrigate the garden in the future.

The walls of the garden facing outwards, denuded of their railings, were only two feet high, except on the north, where there was a drop into the *prés* of several feet, and on the south there was a drop of two feet on the inside. To give more shelter from the wind (not that a wall of any height will keep the mistral out), we built up the wall to six and a half feet on the inner side, putting in entrance doorways on both the south and north sides of the garden. Stone steps led into the garden from the south, and here the door had a moulded stone frame with an architrave and an *œille de bœuf* (peephole) over the heavy

The perron leading to the
north terrace, with the
sphinx and the wall fountain

wooden door; moulded stones curved down to two stone 'ledges' on either side which carry a pair of
stone baskets of fruit from Italy. On the north, because the levels were different, the stone door
surround was simpler. I placed one of the Roman busts above the door.

The collapsed wall at the east end of the garden was more of a problem: it was not easy to imagine
what it had been like originally, so we just had to make a guess. Raising it in the centre to about twelve
feet, we topped it with stone tiles and curved it down to be finished each side by a square of stones with
pineapples on them. We had discovered these in the undergrowth near by, so possibly they might have
formed part of the original composition – a supposition perhaps made more likely because they looked
so comfortable where we placed them.

I had five other Italian stone baskets of fruit and I put two of these on corners of the wall. The third
sat happily where the ornament was missing from the top of the watering and washing basin's fountain
bowl, looking as though it had simply returned home.

There is a story attached to these stone pieces from Italy. They came originally from my great-uncle
Algernon Bourke, who had a business in Pisa and Putney providing stone garden ornaments. He must
have been the most delightful fellow, adored by his family and friends; he was pictured in a Spy cartoon,
a raconteur and wit, who was the subject of many a good story. The only trouble was that, although
equipped with a good eye and perfect taste, he wasn't very good at business, and when the bills came
in to Pisa, he was always in Putney and when they came to Putney, he was always in Pisa; however, it

The perron leading to the
north terrace, with the
sphinx and the wall fountain

seemed that they all got paid in the end. I wish I'd known him. I could have, just, as he died a few years after I was born. The ornaments were given by him to his sister, my great-aunt Florrie, and she left them to my father, who gave them to me.

On the piers of the gate leading to what was to be the north terrace, I put a pair of Italian stone obelisks. The gate was quite a nice plain iron-barred one, which I painted bleu de Versailles, a dark greenish blue-grey, a paint colour we eventually used on all the ironwork.

Now came the moment to mark out the patterns for the beds and borders in the walled garden. We had laid a terrace with limestone slabs, which lay outside the east door, leading from what became the Petit Salon. There was a drop with a five-inch step from the doorway on to the terrace and another of six inches to the garden level. I made narrow borders under the walls of the house, with wider ones under the walls at the east end of the walled garden. The ones under the walls of the house I planted with some roses to climb the walls and white *Clematis montana*.

First I will tell of the design I made for this garden within the walls. As the house was a mid-eighteenth-century one and the space enclosed, it had surely to be formal. Châteaux in the Vaucluse generally had formal gardens, though quite a few had followed the prevailing fashion in the late eighteenth and early nineteenth centuries of having a *jardin à l'Anglaise*. Box (*Buxus sempervirens*), much used for formal parterres in Provençal gardens and growing wild in profusion on the slopes of Mont Ventoux, was what I chose to edge the pattern of beds to be formed within the walls. I will not describe the patterns of the design, as this can be better seen in Derry's photographs, which depict them perfectly.

The first thing I should have done was to have the soil tested. The consequences of not having done so were dire, as will be recounted later, but having been told the garden, in the fairly recent past, had been a properly tended one, planted with roses and other plants, I assumed it would have been well fertilized, and presumably having lain fallow for a considerable time, it should have been in pretty good heart, needing only cleaning, fertilizing and digging over. Never was an assumption so disastrously wrong.

So I proceeded, with much excitement, to choose and plant many old-fashioned roses – Centifolias, Gallicas, Damasks, Teas and Chinas, in eager expectation that I should in a year or two walk about the garden embraced by beauty and scent. My first suspicion that all was not well with the soil came when I found no worms; indeed, when, after several years, I came across my first worm, I was so overjoyed I felt like kissing it. Was the soil dead? The roses looked dreadfully unhappy, stunted and yellow. One by one, or rather four by four, they died; after some years, I counted fifty-six labels that had come off dead roses. No remedies I gave them seemed to please them – sequestrene, horse manure from a local stables, fish, blood and bone, even cow manure with algae. It was like trying to feed an obstinate child who turned its head and clamped its mouth shut: the plants refused to take any remedy to cure their maladies. What could be wrong? I despaired. It was not just the roses: almost everything I planted in perfect health soon turned up its toes. I refused to be defeated I persisted with my efforts, and now at last the plants are looking content, though there are those who still take a jaundiced view of the soil. Lilies thrive and multiply, and I was so pleased to see at last something that liked St Clou that I plant some new species and hybrids each year and am now going to try some in the *prés* and open woodland.

I left one other tree in the walled garden besides the gleditsia (which now, in 2006, has had to be felled, being long past its best) and that was a *Robinia pseudoacacia* with white scented flowers, tall and narrow, growing in the south-west corner and providing some shade for the borders there under the

The abundantly flowering rose 'Rambling Rector' reflected in a *bassin*

Looking down on the geometrically formal pattern composed by the flower-filled box-edged beds of the walled garden on the east of the château. The horizontal lines of the parterre are balanced by the perpendiculars of topiary and tall cypresses and the softer rounded shapes of the planted arches over the paths.

The walled garden with the fountain and the doorway to the south

walls, for the polyanthus, hellebores, lily of the valley and shade-loving plants I have put there. *Wisteria sinensis* and bignonias (the lemon yellow one as well as the deep orange) climb up the high wall above the Roman dolphin at the east end of the garden. Facing them is a round stone table in front of a stone bench, where you can perch for moments to sip a cup of tea or a glass of wine and listen to the trickling water from the emerald-green moss-moustached and bearded Roman dolphin. To the right, there is a curious box tree, leaning out from the base of the wall and huge, at least a hundred years old, and though not of great beauty, of a character that lends an eccentric note to the garden. I have put a large terracotta old jar at its side, which is bang in the centre of the path as you look from the terrace. I planted two pairs of crab apple standards, small-growing ones, which have in the spring white flowers, with deep pink buds, and in autumn deep red apples.

   These brought height where the lines of the parterre were largely horizontal, but still I felt there were too few perpendicular lines, so I planted two Italian cypresses either side of the high east wall and

arches along the cross paths of the parterre. The arches were made of the metal rods put into concrete to strengthen it for building purposes; they were ideal and could be found in many different thicknesses. I painted them lead grey, which I find is kinder to plants than black, and trained olive plants over them. These fruit and flower and look quite delectable until they get much older, when they have to be trimmed twice a year, which is once too many for olives to continue to flower and fruit; pruning once a year in March is all they will put up with.

Looking east across the walled garden

   The box-edged beds near the east end of the château below the stone terrace I planted very formally, the pattern planted with grey and green santolina. The grey was another of my failures, although it grew so well at Hatfield and Cranborne, and it had to be substituted with the silver curry plant (*Helichrysum angustifolium*). In the centre of one bed there was a monogram of crossed Ss and in the centre of the other the letters MS intertwined. Box clipped into pyramids, balls on stems and rounded pillars with knobs on top, with the patterns in the beds outlined in box, completed the parterres.

The grey and green parterre
in the walled garden, planted
with santolina and
Helichrysum angustifolium

The walls were planted with many roses, clematis – chiefly the smaller-flowered ones and Viticella types, honeysuckle, jasmine and trachelospermum, with *Ipomoea* 'Heavenly Blue' and its blue and white sport in the summer, plus a beauty in claret and purple.

On the northern side of the château we made a stone and cobbled terrace with a perron, its steps descending in a curve on either side to the *prés* below. The terrace has beds either side of the steps that lead into the house and narrow ones under the low walls that embrace it. Here I have planted only scented white-flowered plants, white-flowered hostas, green and white *Hydrangea arborescens* 'Annabelle', white hibiscus, white *Lilium speciosum* and the oriental *L.* 'Casa Blanca', *Viola* 'Mrs Lancaster', which enjoys shade, white polyanthus and white-flowered dicentra for spring, when the white tulips and narcissus are flowering.

For climbing up the walls of the house I planted a huge rose with bunches of scented flowers that came from Cranborne, taken from a plant, that is, I think, now out of commerce, a beauty called *Rosa cerascarpa*. There is a scented white *Clematis montana* climbing up the west tower, a dwarf white-flowered alstroemeria, hardly ever out of flower, and a huge plant of my beloved *Rosa × alba* 'Alba Maxima', the origins of which are lost in the mists of time. It must be a tough old thing, for it has survived for centuries, its toughness sometimes taking it through years of neglect. It has been found in long-abandoned old gardens, still gallantly bearing its deliciously scented flowers. Here on the north terrace it flings great arching branches over the top of the gate leading to the walled garden.

I now return to the south front of the château, and to the plantings I made to the west side of the house. There was a narrow bed under the house, edged with a ragged box hedge. I dug this hedge up and replanted it to run from the entrance door of the farmhouse to a yew hedge we planted to screen the house from our neighbour's drive, and also from the narrow road beyond. The box hedge, which is now a good six feet high, is forming arches over the entrances to the herb garden and vegetable patch or *potager*. Here there was a parcel of land, as well as an area of vines, that belonged to our neighbour, which now became a veritable Naboth's vineyard. After several years it came to us, and I was then able to finish the design for the *potager* and herb garden, surrounding the beds with a low rosemary hedge and narrow grass paths. On a dewy morning, or after rain, the scent is delicious, and my little terrier, Bonnie, after hunting mice through those hedges, comes in smelling like a herb cushion.

When this land came in, it opened up several new possibilities. What of the vineyard? Should we keep it or grub up the vines and plant trees? Both had their attractions, but the argument to plant trees won. They would give more privacy and protection from the road; although at the moment there was little traffic on it, that could increase in the future. The decision taken, I made another idiotic mistake. After clearing the vines, instead of taking soil tests and deeply cultivating the ground, and asking for local advice about what to do next, I planted a great many trees. Although I chose trees known to do well in the region, and prepared the sites well, few seemed to thrive, not even the evergreen oak (*Quercus ilex*), which is native to Provence, as are some other oaks, such as *Q. cerris*. However, the limes (*Tilia cordata*) were happy, as were the field maple (*Acer campestre*), various ashes (*Fraxinus*), hawthorn (*Crataegus monogyna*) and wild cherry (*Prunus avium*). A friend gave me three white mulberries (*Morus alba*), the food of silkworms, the manufacture of silk once having been an industry in Provence. Planted in 1988, they flourished and now bear delicious, intensely sweet fruit in May. For the first years there was no irrigation, but, thanks to having natural springs, we were able to introduce it seven years ago, and the failing trees responded like an invalid to a tonic, especially a row of poplars, alternating with evergreen oaks, planted along the road as a screen.

There are rough-mown *allées* between the trees, eight feet wide, three *allées* each way, north to south and east to west, and the trees have been planted to the *allées*. A neighbour told me that in her childhood she remembers carpets of wild cyclamen beneath the evergreen oaks, and when there is enough shade, I hope to reintroduce them; already I have planted many, notably round the boles of the planes lining the entrance drive on the north. In the area of rough grass dotted with mature trees, there are now many anemones, not only *A. blanda* and *A.b.* 'White Splendour', but *A. coronaria* De Caen Group and St Brigid Group, and the delicate white one on a tall stem that never seems out of flower. Even snowdrops seem happy; they do not spread much, but I'm amazed that they grow at all. I remember thinking it was rather eccentric to plant them in Provence, but thank God I did. They are such a joy at the New Year.

When the extra piece of land came in, I was able to move the sixty-year-old olive trees I had planted in the only space then available, where they were in too much shade. I replanted them framing a mown grass walk edged in lavender and enclosed by a fat and high rosemary hedge. In the spaces of grass between the trees, I planted for the autumn the saffron crocus, *C. sativus*, a cloudy purple, its dangling stamens laden with saffron. They are exquisite. (Until the eighteenth century the meadows around Saffron Walden in Essex were sheeted with saffron crocuses, grown chiefly for the dye trade – what a sight it must have been in the autumn!) Under the olive trees, in the spring the species tulip *Tulipa humilis* appears first, looking somewhat like a crocus with its yellow-based lilac-pink flowers, followed by

The olive walk

T. bakeri, which is a rosy lilac colour. With the grey and silver of the olives and the silvers of the lavender, they are a satisfying sight, but there are not as many as there should be by now. We have much trouble with field mice eating the bulbs, indeed any bulbs, but I have discovered a deterrent, and here is the recipe. Buy some cayenne pepper: the quantity you need will depend on how many bulbs you have, but my guess is that you will require a considerable number of packets of the stuff, so I recommend that you go to an Indian shop. Empty the packets into a large bowl or bucket and mix the pepper with water till you have a thickish cream of the right consistency to coat the bulbs. Then plant as usual, laying a curse on the pests and saying a prayer. Since I did this the mice of St Clou have left my bulbs alone.

Another foolishness was not having mugged up about olives. I thought, in my ignorance, that an olive was an olive was an olive; instead, of course, there are many varieties, some suited to certain areas better than others. Of course, I bought the wrong one – 'Nyons' instead of 'Verdale' – my mistake being immediately pointed out to me by a local friend just as I was gazing in pride and joy at the magnificent new arrivals. However, much to my delight, in spite of being in the wrong area and wrong soil, they thrive and their fruits provide some excellent oil.

We built a greenhouse with cold frames attached; indeed we built two greenhouses, because the first one was destroyed in 1992, when a great flood swept down from the foothills of Mont Ventoux across the vineyards carrying all before it – houses, bridges, caravans and cars. Over two hundred people were drowned and in Vaison le Romaine, a town in the Vaucluse, the only bridge that survived was the Roman one. Our river at the bottom of the *prés*, the River Mède, became a raging torrent and the *prés*, with the cascade, became invisible under its waters. It looked very beautiful – I wished it could always look like that. On the southern side of the château another river appeared that with great force and fury poured through the château's ground floor and that of the farmhouse. From a window, I saw a heavy terracotta oil pot from the herb garden sweep past me, carried like a leaf on the surface of the rushing water; and our gardener, trying to make a hole in the wall by the greenhouse to release the water, was overwhelmed by the force of the flood and carried with the greenhouse and all it contained, plus the shattered wall, fifteen feet into the *prés* below. The walled garden of the swimming pool, which was at a lower level, filled up like a tank and the pressure of hundreds of tons of water cracked the stone structure of the pool. However, some good came out of this disaster. After a hot dry summer, the trees and plants were well watered and the flood, having swept away topsoil from the vineyards, left a welcome mulch on the garden.

There is a garden round the swimming pool. Terracotta pots filled with scented geraniums are ranged along the front of the pool house with its stone pillars and sloping roof of old Provençal tiles. There are broad borders either side, filled with roses, that flower from early May into November, sunflowers, dahlias, scented white arabis, pinks, vervain and salvias and two standard clerodendrums, their leaves fetid-smelling but their white, red-calyxed flowers with a glorious scent which accompanies the slowly circulating swimmer. In the corner is a bower made with the same concrete strengtheners, again painted a lead colour. Vines climb over it and the occupants of the hammocks slung below can lift a lazy hand and pick that most delicious of grapes, a Muscat.

I created one more garden, which is known as the Little Garden or Petit Jardin. It is criss-crossed by narrow brick paths, and has a round wooden seat encircling a *Diospyros kaki*, the Chinese persimmon, with edible fruits looking like polished oranges. I have filled the brick-edged beds with tree peonies, with tulips for April and May, lilies for June, August and September, pansies, violas and pinks in abundance, salvias, many of the finds of

The Petit Jardin in summer, with lilies, roses and clematis in flower

the botanist and plant hunter James Compton – again sunflowers, a lemon-coloured one with a coal-black centre, small alliums and, of course, roses, as well as many treasures not in any other part of the garden. The soil is better here and most plants thrive with sun, good food and irrigation.

On the north side of the Petit Jardin, I made a narrow pergola, which runs from a bower looking to the herb and vegetable garden with a view of the château to the olive tree walk. The bower is clad in *Elaeagnus commutata* with creamy, deliciously scented, flowers in May.

Twenty years have passed since we came to St Clou, and though much has been done, there float in my head many ideas and dreams for improvements and additions to the garden and landscape, for what gardener is ever satisfied? I am building a *poullier* for the chickens, with a pointed roof in Provençal tiles with a jaunty cockerel perched on top; and at the west end of the olive walk a belvedere, octagonal in form. This too has a tiled roof; a door faces the walk, and one window looks down the little pergola, one to the *petit forêt* and the fourth across the entrance to a rough grass path leading to a stone obelisk – an object to walk to, to repose in after a *tour des environs*, to read in, to snooze in, even to sleep in on a hot August night. Here will be a skylight so that you can gaze at the starlit sky and the amber-coloured harvest moon.

An oval pool has been added, lying in the raised grass apron in the front of the north entrance to the château, with pillars of clipped yew marching down either side. And I have plans for the winding walk through the oaks and planes by the river. Since the devastating flood, its beauty has been spoilt by the sand and stones deposited in ugly heaps and shoals by the swollen waters. Much clearing of riverbed and pool must be done; the waterfall is half its original height and there is no room for trout.

It is good to have ambitious projects in one's head, even if never fulfilled, fair and golden visions, hope and optimism, although one may only be building castles in the air.

NEWBRIDGE HOUSE

DUBLIN

Alec Cobbe for Fingal County Council

In 1989, I had the lovely prospect of spending some time in Ireland. For me to go there is to feel I am going home – not an entirely reasonable feeling, for although a good deal of my childhood and girlhood was spent in Ireland, only my father was Irish; I can only think I must have many more of my papa's Irish genes than my mother's English ones. An invitation from Alec Cobbe to design a garden for him at Newbridge House, his home near Dublin, was the reason for going there.

Alec is a man of many parts; indeed, to think of him and the wealth of his skills and talents is to be reminded, inevitably, of a man of the Renaissance, cultured, learned in the arts and at the same time a craftsman, able to fashion with his hands, rich in imagination, at once dreamer and creator. To see Alec's transformation of a dirty and damaged picture, to hear him play Bach or Chopin on the clavichord or harpsichord, to watch him paint a seventeenth-century tulip, engrave a crystal glass, design a doll's house, print and illustrate, on an early printing press, a Lilliputian book, or paint a still life, a landscape or an elaborate menu for a banquet is inordinately to admire and to be filled with wonder at such a truly astonishing range of skills and talents. It was a delight to have been asked to design Alec's garden, albeit a challenge too, and I determined that it would be a star garden, something that I hoped would not be ashamed to stand companion with the beauty Alec brings to all he creates.

Below Newbridge House
Opposite Designs for the vegetable and herb gardens

The garden was a walled one, enclosing five acres of land, now lying fallow, and adjacent to the courtyard behind the house. Charles Cobbe, Archbishop of Dublin from 1686 to 1765, had built the house. James Gibbs was the architect, and of the two alternative designs he provided, one was executed. Both designs survive, one being amongst the Cobbe papers and the other bequeathed by the architect to the Radcliffe Library in Oxford. Gibbs also provided designs for chimneypieces, door cases, mouldings and ceilings within the house. Newbridge House is his only work executed in Ireland, and it has been occupied by the Cobbe family ever since it was built. This long occupation by one family has created a palpable atmosphere, at once cosy as well as grand. There is the drawing room with comfortable places to sit and the picture gallery with its original collection of old masters, collected by Thomas and Lady Betty Cobbe, the Archbishop's son and daughter-in-law, and there is a cabinet of curiosities holding everything from a mummified bull's ear to a Tahitian head brought back by Captain Cook. The lives and personalities of those from each generation who lived in the house have surely contributed to the flavour and feeling in the atmosphere that pervades it, as herbs will flavour a dish.

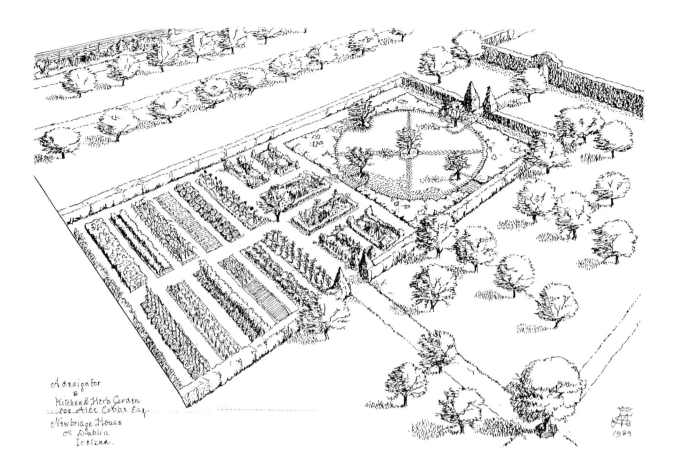

A design for
Kitchen & Herb Garden
for Alec Cobbe Esq.
Newbridge House
Co Dublin
Ireland.

1989

I did what I always do before designing a garden, survey the whole place inside and out, viewing it from the windows of the house at each point of the compass, seeking what is famously called the spirit of the place.

The walled garden at Newbridge was built handily near the house (the access to the house being through a small courtyard on the south and an outbuilding), unlike many late eighteenth-century and nineteenth-century kitchen gardens, which were often inconveniently sited far from where the family lived.

When I first saw Newbridge's walled garden, it had a dismal air of neglect and abandonment. There were a couple of greenhouses which were in a bad way, surrounded by a post and wire fence; three fenced small rectangular enclosures of varied size, called on the survey map provided by the Dublin council 'compounds' (I never discovered why); a ruined part-brick-built summerhouse; and two telegraph poles, which served no purpose as they had no wires attached to them, I was glad to note. There were curtains of ivy and polygonum, long-neglected lilacs, self-sown colonies of ash and sycamore saplings, much spotted laurel (a particular hate of mine, though I have noticed that is creeping back into fashion), brambles and elder bushes, and several largish trees in impossible positions.

However, I was happy to note that there were, against these minuses, a healthy number of pluses. There was a magnificent walnut tree, a huge *Catalpa bignonioides* and many good though long unpruned and shapeless fruit trees, as well some wall fruit, including several fig trees, every one needing attention.

There were also some good features here and there on the walls, including one that could be turned into an attractive place to sit, its central recessed keystoned arch with niches either side perfect for an architectural seat and a pair of classic statues or urns. The feature rose a foot above the wall and was enclosed by square brick half pillars with stone capitals, one with remains, in the shape of a foot and stem, which must have supported a finial, perhaps a stone sphere or a pineapple.

It is eighteen years since I did the designs for the garden at Newbridge, and to refresh my memory I have been reading the papers I wrote with suggestions and proposals for its renovation. Clearing, cutting, pruning and lopping would play a big part at the beginning. An example is some large trees behind the north wall, some of their branches hanging over it and shading the sixteen-foot-wide border I was planning there; these branches had to be removed. The many other invasive weeds and creepers that I have already mentioned, and that had partially taken over the neglected garden, had to be eliminated before the work of drawing up the overall design for it could be begun.

I asked my architect friend if he would help me, and together we worked out how the designs would fit into the five acres with the paths and borders, and the existing trees and architectural features.

All the gardens within the walls were to be enclosed themselves. There was an orchard surrounded by a three-foot-high hornbeam hedge with arched exits and entrances. A kitchen and herb garden was to be laid out to the north of the greenhouses, which were enclosed by an old box hedge. The houses would look good there, but were in need of restoration, and some additional large box plants had to be added to complete the enclosure. There was a very ancient leaning apple tree here, which had to be removed – a character, but sadly hopelessly in the wrong place. The kitchen and herb garden would be enclosed by

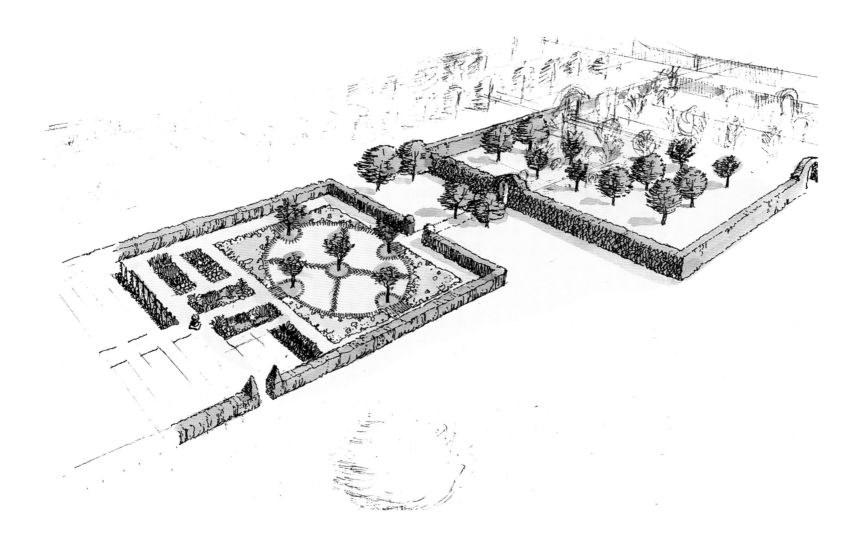

four-foot-high box hedges and the kitchen garden's beds divided by paths laid in brick. The herb garden was to be defined by a circle of brickwork linking four crab apple trees, with one in the centre; four 'paths' of brickwork led to the central crab apple from the circle, leaving the remaining spaces for the herbs.

The kitchen, herb garden and orchard were all to the west, running from south to north, while to the east lay three gardens all bounded by three-foot-high yew hedges and with a central path running from one to another. The southern garden was to grow a mixture of plants and bulbs for all seasons; the centre garden was to be an oval-shaped scented garden, and the garden to the north a garden of roses of the old-fashioned kind with names like 'Maiden's Blush' and 'Cuisse de Nymphe' underplanted with pinks with equally evocative names – 'Painted Lady', 'Queen of Sheba', 'Pheasant's Eye'. The garden of mixed plantings would have a sundial in its centre, by great good fortune one made for Newbridge from a design by James Gibbs.

There were avenues planted with apple trees on both sides of the garden, running from south to north, and a similar one down the middle of the garden, each with a central gravel path. Some of the apple trees were missing, and had to be replanted, and all needed pruning and shaping, but with these

Above Design for a herb garden and an orchard
Opposite, above Design for a seat and niches in the walled garden
Opposite, below Design for an orchard and avenue of fruit trees in the kitchen garden

1

2

3

attentions carried out the framing of the gardens with walls, borders, paths and avenues would be complete, and the planting of the flower, fruit, herb and vegetable gardens within this frame would create the picture.

Newbridge House and grounds are maintained and opened to the public by Fingal County Council, who have not yet carried out these plans but may do so one day. So perhaps I will be able to walk in the gardens before I die. What an excitement and pleasure that would be.

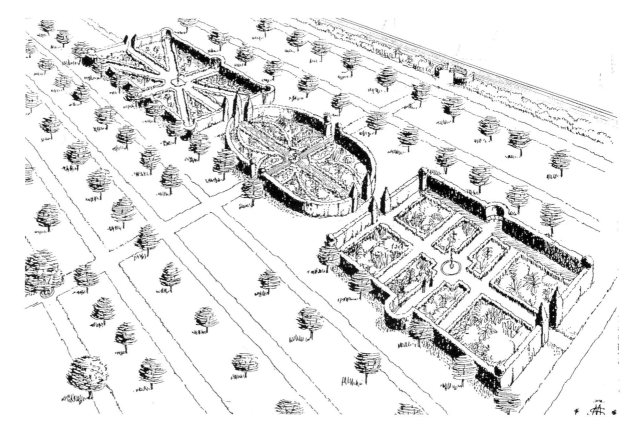

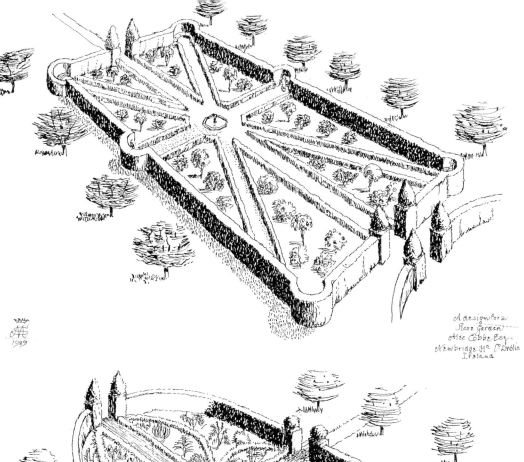

Designs for (clockwise from far left, top): the main entrance to the garden; a garden of roses; a scented garden; a flower garden; an assembly of the three, with avenues of fruit trees; various types of garden house

A design for a
Rose Garden
Alec Cobbe Esq.
Newbridge H^e Co Dublin
Ireland

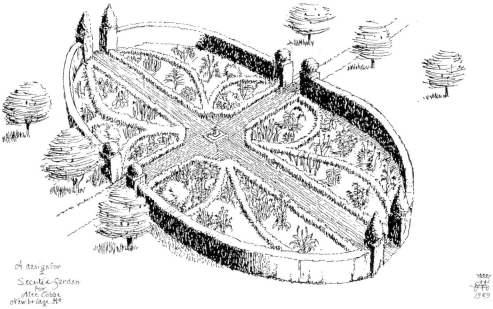

A design for
Scented Garden
for
Alec Cobbe
Newbridge H^e

1989

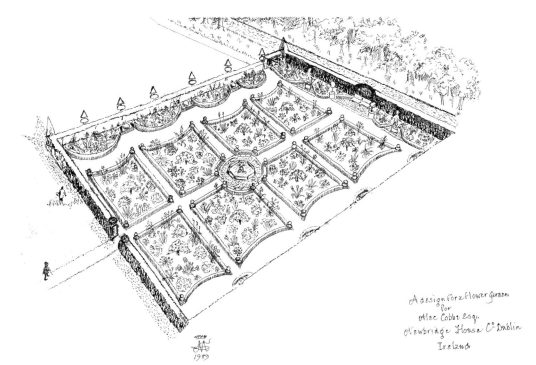

A design for a Flower Garden
for
Alec Cobbe Esq.
Newbridge House Co Dublin
Ireland

1989

CASTLETOWN COX

COUNTY KILKENNY

George Magan

The story of how I became involved in the designing of the gardens at Castletown was rather an unusual and romantic one. It came about like this. I was reading in my house in Provence early one morning when the courier arrived, and amongst my post was a letter from a George Magan. He wrote that he had bought a house in Ireland, in County Kilkenny, called Castletown, that he knew my connection with this house, that he had seen the gardens I had designed at Hatfield and that he wondered if I would consider designing the gardens at Castletown. Castletown was a name that awoke for me a magical world: the world of my early childhood, peopled with my Irish family, an adored grandmother and grandfather, and occasional visits from a sailor father, not to speak of an aunt who always made me laugh. The answer to this invitation was, perhaps not unexpectedly, yes. There was a plane at Avignon and I flew for the day to Waterford.

My all-too-infrequent visits to Ireland were always accompanied by a sensation of 'going home' and this visit was no exception. Indeed, I felt the sensation even more strongly. Castletown had been my grandparents' and their children's home since 1909. With my two sisters, I had my day and night nurseries on the top floor, and we were woken most mornings by the noise of Old Shooney, the house carpenter, stomping up the uncarpeted wooden stairs in his boots to carry out mysterious jobs in the upper storey. A much-loved Irish nanny, Nanny Vincent, and a cosy, fat nursery maid, Ethel, looked after us. Nannies always seemed to have a letter to post, so many an afternoon was spent driving to Carrick-on-Suir, the local town, in our donkey cart, my little sister, still in long clothes (you weren't – as it was called – 'shortened' till you were three months old), in the umbrella box. I can still see her little face, with its piercing deep Irish blue eyes, looking up at me, framed by her lace and lawn bonnet. When we arrived at the post office, the donkey invariably lay down, and it was only through the energetic action of several local men loitering by the post office with their 'ash plants' that it was persuaded, by encouraging whacking, to get to its feet. In retrospect I think it must have, rather masochistically, enjoyed this attention, as it lay down on every visit to the post office.

When I regaled my host – who had met me at the airport and was driving me to Castletown – with this memory, I was touched to be asked, 'Would you like to go and see the post office?' And there it was, in every particular the same – same paint, green and red, same door, same window. Much had changed in Ireland over the fifty years that had passed, but not the post office in Carrick-on-Suir. Only the men with the ash plants were missing.

Castletown was built by Michael Cox, Archbishop of Cashel, in 1767. His wish was to have a home which reflected the importance of his station, and the resultant building must have amply achieved his

Looking north-west over the box parterres and the hornbeam and evergreen oak walks

I designed the reflecting pool to complement the simple grandeur of the house.

wish. Castletown Connolly may be the most famous of Ireland's many beautiful houses but Castletown Cox wins the palm as the loveliest. The Archbishop is said to have claimed he was to build a small house and a large church; however, what came out was a large house and very small church. The church was the scene of a childhood humiliation for me at the age of four or five. Told by my aunt that I must join in the hymns and sing at the first note of the organ, I burst into 'Baa baa black sheep' at the top of my small voice. This was the only song I knew; and in spite of adult fingers to lips, and multiple shushings, I carried on feeling I was obeying orders and was removed, protesting loudly that I had only done what I'd been told to do. I can still remember the rage I felt at the unfairness of it.

The Archbishop chose as his architect a man of French-Italian descent, Daviso d'Arcort. He was an architect-engineer and came to Ireland in the mid-eighteenth century, becoming known there as Davis Ducart. Castletown Cox is his masterpiece. It sits with its arcades and pavilion with their cupolas stretching east and west from the main block of the house, which is built in limestone and unpolished Kilkenny marble. It is an improbably perfect composition, constructed on level ground terraced down to a ha-ha and looking out over the undulations of the demesne, where cattle and sheep quietly graze, above the valley of the river Suir, and beyond to the astonishing beauty of the Comeragh mountains and Slievenamon.

The trees are magnificent, largely oaks, many very ancient, possibly the result of natural regeneration from part of a primeval forest, and George Magan has planted over 100,000 more trees in avenues and mixed woodlands.

Such was the setting for the garden I had been asked to create. The task was going to be both exciting and challenging, and so it has proved. To work somewhere that I had already affection for, and only happy memories of (always excepting the incident in the church), was something rare and special. I had too a sympathy for the family I was to work for, because my family, like theirs, was, as my Irish relations called it, 'proper Irish' – no Anglo-Irish nonsense or, as my husband expressed it, 'bog Irish', though he too had many drops of Irish blood. The Magan family had their seat in Co. Westmeath, and legend has it that they had once been able to drive their cattle from one side of Ireland to the other, all on their own land. Much to the family's sorrow, their house and demesne had to be sold in 1967. George's mother told me that at the age of eleven he vowed that one day he would re-establish the family in Ireland. With the acquisition of Castletown, his vow had been realized.

On my first visit there in my new role, I did an exhaustive tour of the surroundings of the house, while looking out over the demesne and the views beyond from the east, west and south. On the north, the entrance side, there was no distant view. Here you looked across an expanse of mown and wild grass, past some very fine, tall and broad oaks to the woods beyond, backed by low hills.

I went into the house as well, to look out from its windows on to each aspect, which helped me a great deal to absorb the feel and spirit of the place. Within the rooms and staircase, some of the finest plasterwork in existence covers ceilings and walls; it was created by Irish craftsmen from Cork, whose skills might have been taught them by an Italian stuccoist. Years of repainting had thickened and

A view east over two of the four box parterres next to the house and the east walk of mop-headed evergreen oaks

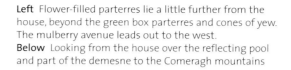

Left Flower-filled parterres lie a little further from the house, beyond the green box parterres and cones of yew. The mulberry avenue leads out to the west.
Below Looking from the house over the reflecting pool and part of the demesne to the Comeragh mountains

blunted the original sharpness of detail and one of Castletown's owners, a master of the local hounds, the Ballymacad, while dining with hunting companions after a good day's sport, amused himself by shooting off the heads of the ho-ho buds on the ceiling. So a lot of slow and delicate repairs had to be carried out to restore the plasterwork to its original beauty.

What was especially striking was that in spite of, or because of, the perfection of the house's architecture, and some elaboration of detail, such as the fluted Corinthian pilasters and the cupolas and fishscale tiles on the pavilions, the whole composition had an overall simplicity, integral with its surroundings. I felt that whatever I designed should not disturb this simplicity and integration but continue to develop both, so that the final result would be a house and garden melded into a single indivisible whole, the relationship between the two of them being like that between a precious stone and its setting. David Brown writes in his book *God and the Enchantment of Place* that gardening and painting have strongly influenced each other. In both a strong focus on simplicity can be aesthetically pleasing. In most successful garden designs there is an attempt to integrate house and garden into a single whole.

So: no fussiness, not too many flowers near the house, stone, green and water. I designed two stone fountains, one for the west and one for the east of the house. The green of box, yew and phillyrea, fountains and a pool, combined with evergreen oaks (*Quercus ilex*), to create an air of tranquillity

Right Plan for the layout of the garden on the west of the house
Below Looking west to Slievenamon over a box parterre, a fine evergreen oak (*Quercus ilex*), and the mulberry and hornbeam avenues

and peace. Some trees in formal positions defined by containing hedges and paths; a wild garden with mown-grass paths, for largely spring-flowering trees and bulbs; and eventually a walled kitchen garden. My grandparents' kitchen garden was far from the house, as was usual in the old days. With a smaller number of gardeners to bring in the vegetables, flowers and pots for the house, it was no longer agreeable or practical to have it so far away. No one wants to walk a quarter of a mile to pick a pea or to carry back a flowering plant.

One of my great pleasures in working on the design of the gardens at Castletown has been to discuss ideas and plans with George Magan's mother, a very experienced gardener. We have worked closely together over these years, now nearly fourteen, and it is seldom that we have not been in agreement. The enjoyment of the work has been much enhanced by having her at my side with her great taste and knowledge.

There is still much to be done, even after all these years – designs for the east and west sides of the reflecting pool, a walled garden and a scheme for a swimming pool garden (that I have already designed but that has not yet been realized).

I also have a dream that I much hope will one day become a reality: a garden pavilion, its architecture harking back to the mysterious round towers of Ireland, the purpose of which has been guessed at but is not altogether certain. It would be open to all the views at ground level and have a room with a fireplace and windows facing north, south, east and west, reached by a spiral staircase. Here you could write a poem, have a meal, read a book. You could look into the garden towards Slievenamon, the

Below Plan of a design for the south of the house, not yet entirely realized

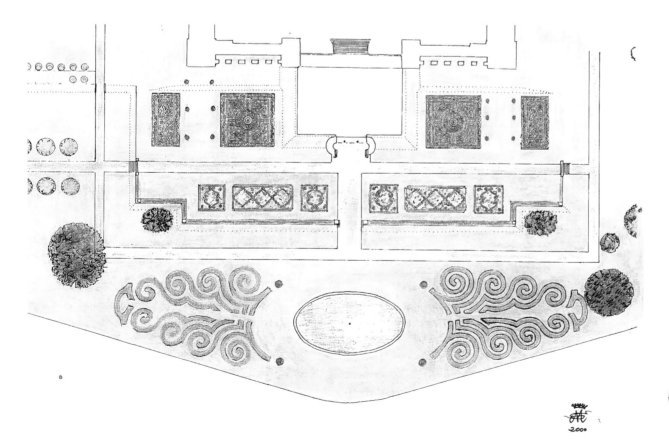

Above left A stone bench
on a grassy stepped pedestal
Above right Fountain and
statues in the green shade
Below Designs for
decorative seating

A design for Castletown Cox's Garden   Stone seat facing south

mountain of fairies and leprechauns, where cars go backwards up hill with the engine switched off, and where a little shoe was found that no human hand could have fashioned, its workmanship so unmanlike that it convinced my robust and normally sceptical aunt that leprechauns did exist. From another window you could look at the Comeragh mountains with the evening sun beginning to set behind them, to the east on to fine woods, and to yet more trees in the woods rising on the hillsides to the north.

Now the gardens have their flower parterres, their yew hedges, fountains and statues, some from Clerwell, my grandparents' other home in Gloucestershire, some newly carved by the immensely talented sculptor Tim Lees. There are roses on the pillars of the arcades, and a wild garden to the west with magnolia, spring and autumn bulbs, malus, prunus and unusual ornamental trees. There are two walks of mop-headed *Quercus ilex*, and a walk of hornbeam (*Carpinus betulus* 'Columnnaris'), backed by a low yew hedge with a pedestalled urn at the end of the vista, as well as a mulberry avenue, which is already fruiting to provide mulberries for jelly and for mulberry ice cream, a delectable summer dish.

Perhaps by the time the gardens at Castletown come to be finished, I shall be under the sod myself, like the roots of the trees I have planted, but I hope I will be able to look down on to the green of the gardens and remember walking there together with my grandmother, looking at the box parterre she had created. During the making of it, she had spent a morning with Paddy, the head gardener, designing it. At one

Left The arcade and the east pavilion, with part of the box and flower parterre and, beyond, the evergreen oak walk
Right, top to bottom Part of the box and flower parterre in summer; the parterre and an early-eighteenth-century Italian statue from Clerwell; climbing roses on the pillars of the arcade

Right A glimpse of the west end of the house at the end of the hornbeam walk
Opposite, above The plan of the main green box parterres
Opposite, below Each of the box parterres leads to an arcade with bay (*Laurus nobilis*) pyramids in oak boxes. Pale apricot roses climb the pillars between.
Below The evergreen oak walk on the west of the house

point, my grandmother left to have lunch, leaving Paddy with instructions to find and mark the centre of the circle in the heart of the parterre. 'Well, Paddy,' she said, on returning, 'have you found it?' 'No, milady,' was Paddy's reply, 'this circle has no centre.'

Perhaps, too, I will glimpse from above the patterns of the designs I have made, and see the trees grown, the stone of the statues and fountains worn by time and weather, the house unchanged; and I would hope not to feel a need to slip down out of the clouds, dissatisfied with what I saw, to adjust some glaring fault of design, but to leave instead a small piece of my heart in the soil I have loved since my earliest childhood.

PETERSHAM LODGE

SURREY

Prince and Princess Rupert Loewenstein

In 1997, Princess Rupert Loewenstein got in touch with me, and asked if I would go and see her garden with a view to redesigning it. Her father had been an old friend of my husband's before our marriage and afterwards of mine too. They had both been officers in the Grenadier Guards and, in the years immediately after the war, her father used to come and stay with us at the Lodge House in the park at Hatfield. I much looked forward to again meeting his daughter, whom we had seen from time to time in the intervening years. One beautiful spring day I motored to Petersham Lodge. I remember seeing from the lane the *Clematis armandii* that festooned the wall enclosing the Lodge's garden and was in full bloom, and the delicious scent from its flowers surrounding me as I entered the house.

Petersham Lodge was built somewhere between 1741 and 1745. The history of the area is rather a confusing one, as there were two estates there and no fewer than four houses called Petersham Lodge. The one where I worked on the garden is on River Lane. The owner of Petersham Lodge in the eighteenth century was a Robert Ord, who had the impressive title of Lord Chief Baron of Scotland, and from then on most of the names of the Lodge's owners were recorded. In 1987 Prince and Princess Loewenstein came to live here and it was ten years later, in 1997, that I was asked to work on their garden.

The space to be redesigned was not a very large one. The house looked south, and had a lawn sloping down towards some very fine trees and a lake with near by a temple or pavilion. The trees screened the house from the bracken-covered slopes and undulations of Richmond Park, with its ancient oak trees and herds of red deer. The garden was cut off and protected from the depredations of the deer and rabbits by a low wire fence, and there was a gate that led from the garden into the park.

Many small trees and shrubs, rhododendrons, viburnums and such-like, clustered around and rose up the trunks of great specimens of forest trees, mainly beech, on the garden side of the fence. The lawn sloped down from a partly paved and narrow box-edged border beneath the southern façade of the lodge. Paired pleached limes were planted from the house halfway down the lawn on the eastern side, but on the west there was no matching lime *allée*. In front of the limes was a rather large pine tree.

This conifer was not happily placed, as it partially screened the formally planted limes and would almost certainly, as it grew, gradually overwhelm them. I suggested that it should be moved to a more suitable site. There were obvious risks in moving it, as it had been planted several years earlier, but I advised that, provided sensible preparations were made, the tree should have a good chance of survival. A big hole must be prepared, large and deep enough to contain the roots, well spread out, and the tree must be thoroughly sprayed with an antitranspirant liquid (to prevent it from transpiring through its foliage), and have some microrrhiza mixed with a good topsoil put around its roots. Such a move should be carried out as swiftly as possible and the tree kept well watered and fed with a good organic fertilizer, such as fish, blood and bone, for at least the next couple of years, until it started growing again.

On the west side of the house, I would have liked to plant another *allée* of limes to match those to the east, so forming a frame for the southern face of the house looking over the lawn to the lake.

I made these suggestions in a prospectus I wrote and sent to the Princess after my first visit to the garden, and will continue now to quote from it.

'If the façade of the house were to be framed by the pleached limes, from the terrace your eye would be drawn down to the splendid tree below the lawn . . . it would be a nice and practical feature to have a simple architectural wooden seat built around this immense and elegantly furnished tree [it is a hornbeam (*Carpinus betulus*), one of the largest and finest I have ever seen].

'I feel there would be a transformation of the view from the terrace if the trees seen from there could be cleared of all the shrubs, bushes and small trees screening their fine trunks.

'The cleared ground could be sown with a short, shade-tolerant grass, red fescue (*Festuca rubra*) and planted with many of the flowers of spring – crocus, anemones, primroses, cowslips, *Cyclamen coum*, dog's-tooth violets and erythroniums in variety, not forgetting snowdrops for the early part of the year in late January and February, with in the autumn *Cyclamen hederifolium* and *Crocus sativus*, the saffron crocus, as well as others of the autumn-flowering crocus such as *C. speciosus*.

'Where the wire fence rises behind the trees, the ground could be cleared to allow for the planting of a hedge, just above the height of the wire. I would suggest the hedge should be of hornbeam and that it should be clipped into arches over the gateways that lead to the wild garden.

'With these suggestions carried out, there would seem to be little else to do, apart from repositioning the planting here and there, because already the garden has some delightful walks, its box parterre and its lake.'

The Princess tells me most of these suggestions were carried out. The big pine tree has gone. However, the *allée* of limes I had felt should be on the east, to match the one already growing on the west, has not been planted. There was a family wedding, the space was needed for the marquee, and might, it was felt, be required again. So the limes had to go by the board, as it were – first things first!

A design for the garden at Petersham Lodge, showing how the suggested *allée* of limes on the west side of the house might match that to the east, framing the southern face of the house

WHITE BIRCH FARM

CONNECTICUT

Peter Brant

The southern face of the
house . The terrace and beds
are punctuated with
elongated domes and
stepped squares of box.

I had a very sketchy acquaintance with the United States when, in 1996, I was asked to design a garden there. I had made a whistlestop tour with my husband on business, which took us first to Fort Lauderdale, then on to Dallas and Kansas and, when business was over, a flight to California to stay with an old American friend from my husband's university days when they were both at Christ Church, Oxford, together, who now lived in Beverley Hills. Our friend gave a dinner for us, at which we met some famous stars; we drove along the Hollywood boulevards and toured the Getty Museum and the Huntingdon Library; and we were taken to see a large Japanese garden on the slope of a hill which made me feel, as Japanese gardens always do, that the only place for them to be is in Japan.

My second visit to the States was when I went to New York, Washington and Philadelphia while giving a series of lectures on behalf of the Museum of Garden History (see page 186), supporting friends of the Tradescant Trust in America. One of my lectures was at Mount Vernon, Washington's old home, and very pretty it was, much smaller and simpler than I expected, with a garden full of boxwood.

The garden I was asked to design was in Connecticut, in the west of the state, fifty minutes' drive from New York and not far from Greenwich. A niece of a great friend of mine had recommended me as a landscape and garden designer to Mr and Mrs Brant, the owners of a 300-acre estate called White Birch Farm. They had never, as far as I knew, seen anything I had done and I feel they were exceedingly trusting to take me on. Now ten years later, I am still designing for them. During those ten years of work, there has not been, for me, a dull moment, and there have been several unusual surprise arrivals in the landscape and garden that my imagination had not catered for.

The park (as we would call it in England) that surrounds the house and formal gardens unfolds towards the south, from a grass terrace and grassed slopes descending towards two great lakes, which have been enlarged but were formed by natural springs, and have tall jets of water, some ten feet or more high, that fling themselves into the air and fall with a restless sound. The lakes are alive with life. There are frogs and fish, Canada geese by the hundred, water-loving insects and, of course, trees that enjoy their roots being damp or even in the water, such as the swamp cypress (*Taxodium distichum*), which grows what we call 'knees' above the water. It is deciduous, striking and beautiful, and turns a yellow bronze in the autumn. These trees we planted near or around the lakes, along with willows, and swamp cypress (*Metasequoia glyptostroboides*), a delicious amber pink in autumn, their trunks shaggy with cinnamon bark.

One of the lakes, with plantings of white-trunked birches

This living relic of a fossil genus was discovered in a village in central China in the early 1940s and arrived in Britain in 1941, and it was much cosseted and fussed over. I remember a bundle of baby ones arriving at Cranborne in the late forties as a present for my father-in-law, from a very grand and famous arboriculturist friend of his, and being in terror in case I did the wrong thing with them till the moment I could pass them into a pair of hands more expert than mine. In the event, they were discovered to be extremely hardy and undemanding.

Other trees we planted about the lakes at White Birch were *Cercidiphyllum japonicum*, which scents the air in autumn with the sweet and pungent smell of burnt sugar, pin oak (*Quercus palustris*), a native tree in the eastern United States, with elegant drooping branches and good autumn colour, and in the drier spots a grove of *Platanus* × *hispanica*. Peter Brant has not only an interest in and knowledge of modern art but also a love of trees, and the two not infrequently get involved with each other, as we shall see later.

In all, 500 trees of many different species and cultivars have been planted on the farm, many hundred during the years I have been working there. They were all planted as large specimens, seldom less than fifteen or twenty feet high, some larger. This took a bit of new thinking. I had been accustomed to planting clumps, groves, woods or avenues with trees seldom more than six feet high, having been taught that at this size they would grow quicker and last longer; we planted for posterity.

Hardly had I arrived before I was taught a lesson in the new thinking. Coming through the entrance gate to White Birch, I noticed that the long winding drive, which traversed the horse paddocks, farm, stables and polo grounds, was bare of trees. How nice it would be, I thought, to have an avenue along its whole length! I mentioned this thought to Peter Brant and almost at once huge lorries arrived with forest trees, their giant rootballs wrapped in burlap; heaps of topsoil, microrrhiza, men with spades and digging machines appeared, and at my next visit I bowled down the drive through an avenue of mature sugar maples. It seemed the stuff of fairy tales. I soon became accustomed to the creation of instant landscape, and thought how Capability Brown and his patrons would have relished it. Of course, it had been done in the distant past, notably at Versailles, but I think never so swiftly achieved. Beeches, cedars of Lebanon, oaks, planes and tulip trees transformed the parkland into a panorama well furnished and looking as though planted a generation ago.

I planted along the borders of the lake (because they too liked damp places), the marsh marigold and *Narcissus poeticus*, which both must have moisture in the spring to flower well.

A broad band of grass, very wide and of an even width, rises up from the main lake, separating two blocks of woodland and sweeping upwards to end in a low hill with a backdrop of trees. Here I suggested there should be a bold 'feature' – an obelisk, a column to mark a person or event, a belvedere or a temple. However, nothing so classic or conventional was considered.

On my next visit to carry out planting and designing at White Birch, I happened, at an early hour in the morning, to look out of the guesthouse where I was staying to see a strange sight. There was a cluster of at least twenty people milling about an enormous object, which turned out to be the sculptor Jeff Koons' *Puppy*. Jeff Koons himself was seated in the bucket seat of a mechanical 'arm', directing the planting of 50,000 annuals all over it. *Puppy* is one of his most sensational creations and had until then been sitting outside the Rockefeller Centre in New York; in Bilbao in Spain there is a second one.

Jeff Koons' *Puppy*

Hundreds of boxes filled with annuals were scattered over the grass; gardeners were on ladders putting the plants into earth-filled holes in wire netting, the outer wrapping in which the body of the puppy was enrobed. The enormous *Puppy* sat on its large bottom and there was a little door between its front legs, which was the entrance to its innards, where a maze of iron pipes contained the irrigation system within the frame. The sight of the elaborate creation of this early-twenty-first-century sculpture was astonishing to watch. Its adorning completed, it was transported, heaven knows how (alas, I missed this historic sight), and I next saw the *Puppy* sitting on the low hill where I had imagined something quite else. Seeing it, as I have, in changing lights and seasons, evergreen in winter and in full bloom in spring and summer, I have quite fallen in love with it. It is a fantasy, with eccentricity and charm and a certain mad suitability.

The house at White Birch was built between 1980 and 1982 and its design, by the architects Alan Greenberg, Ted Johnson and Peter Marina, was influenced by that of Washington's house, Mount Vernon. It has a fine position, high but surrounded by flat ground, except to the west where there is a pool garden and on the south where there is a terraced piece of land I have already described as falling away to the lakes below.

Russell Page was the designer of the layout, the stonework and the gardens surrounding the house, as well as the entrance courtyard, but he declined to do the detailed planting, which was later done by Deborah Nevins. Page was working on several projects then, but his health was starting to fail and he did no further work at White Birch. The forecourt he designed is enclosed by tall yew hedges with a double row of pleached linden trees (*Tilia*) framing the front door of the house and a single tall tulip tree (*Liriodendron tulipifera*) in the centre of the space. It was a challenge to continue designing the landscape and gardens at White Birch, to pick up where Page had had to stop and to try to imagine, when problems and puzzles arose, what solutions he, a master of the art of garden and landscape design, would have found for them; but though a challenge it was an immensely enjoyable one, and after ten years of designing and planting there, the work at White Birch goes on.

White Birch Farm gets its name from the tall, snowy multi-trunked birch trees that line the entrance drive. I suggested the planting should be continued as far as the borders of the lakes, and also as a copse by one of the lakes, taking the place of a large and ugly old vegetable patch, which did nothing for the lake area. I also thought how good sheets of snowdrops would look growing in the grass under the birches, and the bulbs were planted in the early autumn.

As always, I had first discovered as much as I could about the soil and climate. The soil was both clay and loamy. East Connecticut is in zone 5, which means it is hot for three months (any damage at White Birch as the result of this heat, though, is somewhat tempered by irrigation); mild for five months; and

The grove of white-trunked birches

cold with snow and frosts for four months. Many desirable plants cannot tolerate this climate. Roses can be killed, even ones we consider hardy; boxwood is wrapped in burlap in the winter and hedges are protected by wire against the depredations of hungry deer. Any suggestions I made for plantings of sheets of crocus and other plants and bulbs had to be abandoned because of the appetite in winter of these creatures, which no one was allowed to shoot. Altogether I had a lot to learn and many adjustments to make to my early ideas for the plants I could use.

However, I finally got down to active work in March 1997 and planned and planted two areas of the garden. One was the place where a swimming pool was to be built within a flower garden enclosed by yew hedges; there was a pool house, fronted by a stone terrace with curved steps that led down to where the pool was to be, and on this terrace was a tall sculpture by Julian Schnabel. Another garden, quite different in character, was also to be a flower garden; this was on the east side of the house and became known as the Little Garden. It was enclosed on one side by the house, on two sides by a white picket fence and on the remaining side, facing west, a wall made of the local field stone, a form of sandstone

varying in colour from light and dark grey to creamy tones. There was only grass in these spaces when I first saw them, but a year later the Little Garden had eight square boxwood-edged beds with large egg-shaped boxwood topiaries in them and these were soon packed full of roses, lilies, pinks, violas and peonies, and plants and bulbs that would give interest and colour in as many months of the year as is possible in this climate. The beds had stone setts (Belgium blocks) around their edges, which raised them a few inches, and more blocks laid flat to the upright ones, outlining the grass paths and surrounding three circles of grass planted in their centres with standard crab apples, on a medium stock to keep them low. These had the prettiest pink-budded white flowers, and red fruits in the autumn. Two white-painted seats, one against the wall and one against the fence facing south, had metal arches over them, planted with roses and clematis.

I made a long bed running up to the kitchen door, in which grew a collection of herbs, nice and handy for the cook, with three small box wood pyramids set along its centre. At the foot of the white picket fence low thick bushes of alpine strawberries grew, and the narrow borders running down the edges of

Two views of the Little Garden. Eight squares are filled with flowering plants – in spring, tulips and other bulbs – and decorated with elongated boxwood domes. Where four corners meet are circles, defined by setts, each with a central standard crab apple, seen here in blossom.

Right The view from the Little Garden to the east face of the house and the long herb bed by the back door
Opposite The South Lawn with topiaried boxwood standing sentinel behind the sphinxes at the top of the steps

the limestone flagged paths, leading to the gates and house door, were planted with lavender, with some topiary at certain points. The simple white-painted east front of the house now looked down on and formed a charming backcloth to a garden that had become something of a typical cottage one.

I next turned my attention to the area to the south of the house, where there was a large flat lawn with a double row of linden trees at either end. A low stone wall surrounded this space and stone steps led down on to a grass terrace. On the wall either side of the steps, a pair of George III carved stone sphinxes were placed. These legendary protectors of Arcadia had been found in London by Peter Brant and I paid a visit to see them before they came to White Birch.

Right The sphinxes looking out over the vista to the park, lakes, woods and *Puppy*

There was plenty to do to furnish the terrace. The borders either side of the steps were too wide and needed complete replanting, while the flight of steps needed some changes. I sealed the ends of the borders with high rounded lumps of boxwood, divided them with paths leading to seats hedged with *Sarcococca hookeriana* var. *humilis*, a plant flowering in winter with a delicious scent. Simple ornamental terracotta pots went either side of the seats, planted with *Trachelospermum jasminoides*, and squares of boxwood (clipped in diminishing steps) were planted in the borders at each corner of the entrance paths. I wanted to do away with much of the herbaceous stuff, which endlessly repeated itself, and I put in English roses, tree peonies, daphnes, hardy geraniums, species lilies, *Hydrangea arborescens* 'Grandiflora' and, in a more shaded end of one border, hostas, hellebores, lily of the valley and some ferns. Stephanie Brant, a great beauty who looked fragile as porcelain, loved to do the digging and planting and proved to be as strong as Miss Jekyll's boots. We did, between us, a good deal of the planting in these borders.

Two other gardens I tackled now, the pool garden and a walled kitchen garden, having first designed and completed a grass-covered mount, topped by a summerhouse, overlooking the tennis court. Here I planted hornbeam hedges (*Carpinus betulis*), which would grow tall enough to disguise the ugly metal wire round the court and to create a backdrop to the mount and summerhouse.

The main house is connected to the wings by curved arcades, which are open in the warm weather and closed in winter. The west wing has in it an indoor pool and faces, with its façade of white weatherboard and pretty windows, on to a stone terrace. This has a pair of rectangular beds designed by Russell Page, who planted them with alpine pinks which never flourished and have been replaced. There is a large sculpture by Julian Schnabel, *Gradira*, which dominates the terrace, and a set of curved stone steps leading to the swimming pool, which was designed to have a flat stone edge and to be painted a chestnut-brown colour, which oddly enough gives the water deep, dark blue, and shadowy paler blue tones not unlike (I know because I have swum in them) the waters of the Black Sea. The garden was enclosed by yew hedges, but not entirely; it was too open on the east and west, and more yews were planted here along the sides of the terrace, with a narrow entrance gate in white painted wood, to give a greater feeling of enclosure and privacy. At the far end of the pool, a circular recess was

Path between hornbeam hedge & Mount

Hornbeam Hedge

Towered pillars & finials

this grass though not necessary but aesthetically pleasing

Hornbeam hedge surrounding tennis court

Above A design for the summerhouse on the mount and the hornbeam hedge
Left The regular steps of the mount are softened by a carpeting of grass

made in a tapestry of hedges in yew and boxwood, and a narrow entrance not yet fully grown reveals a lead sculpture by Julian Schnabel of a beautiful woman whose body is a curving panel. One day her sorrowing eyes may weep tears that will course down her body and fall into a pool below.

The grass paths bordering the pool edge the borders under the yew hedges, and although they have tulips in the spring, they are mainly planted to flower in the high summer months. Hollyhocks, English roses, late irises, lilies, lavender, rosemary in pots (it has to be brought in for the winter), hardy geraniums, violas, pansies and pinks were amongst the plants chosen, and a colour spectrum was decided on which knocked out bright yellows, orange, violent reds and shocking pinks. It was a restful palette, which included some greys and evergreens – sympathetic, perhaps, to lazy hours on long chairs in the sun.

Stephanie Brant was keen to have a kitchen garden where she could grow her own fruit and vegetables. The possibility of having one became a more practical proposition with the arrival of a head gardener at White Birch, Stuart Moureau, who was experienced and knowledgeable, and I was given the go-ahead to design one. The obvious place was an area above the Little Garden. It was comparatively flat and open to the sun on three sides, with a grove of white Eastern pine trees (*Pinus strobus*) to the north. The space allotted was 8 feet by 120 feet.

Stone walls matching the one in the Little Garden were built and a robust and effective archway led into the kitchen garden, up stone steps from the Little Garden to the higher level. The garden was designed to have narrow beds under the walls, where espaliered fruit trees were planted. There

Opposite Julian Schnabel's sculpture on the terrace above the steps to the swimming pool garden
Below Design for the entrance to the swimming pool garden from the south
Bottom Design for the swimming pool garden with a tall box and yew hedge enclosing the pool and a glimpse of the sculpture at the end

A proposal for the South Lawn

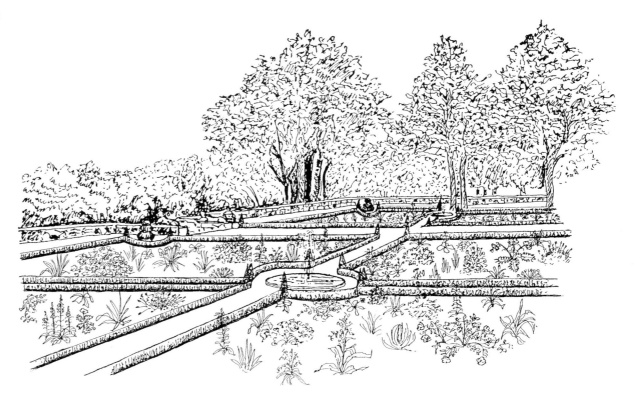

was an octagonal-shaped fountain in the centre, edged with flat stones and surrounded by a cobbled circle. The fountain had a simple single jet of water. There were twenty beds in all for the vegetables and soft fruit, with some room to grow flowers and bulbs for cutting for the house. Twelve rectangular beds, six either side of the fountain, were in the centre, with eight long narrow beds to the east and west. Each bed was raised and outlined by Belgian blocks with more blocks laid flat against them, while the paths were covered in fine gravel made from the same stone, so all the stone, including the cobbles, was in harmony.

The final addition to the garden, or the last but one, was a pergola of metal, painted in bleu de Versailles and covered with climbing roses and clematis. 'Iceberg' is one rose, 'Eden Rose' another, and there will be more added, as well as the honeysuckle *Lonicera periclymenum* 'Graham Thomas', a particularly good form of *L. periclymenum*, *L. × italica* and *Caprifolium × etrusca*, *Clematis flammula* for scent in late summer and *C. rubra* 'Marginata', plus some *C. viticella* hybrids. A white rose, probably 'Wedding Day', and *Wisteria sinensis* 'Alba' will cover the metal canopy mounted over the fountain.

There is already fruit on the walls, and there are currants and gooseberries in the beds. Such a *potager*, with its orderly rows of blue-grey cabbages as stiff and blue as the leaves of the leeks, the brilliance of the green in parsley and curly kale, the improbable colours – yellow, ambers, flaming pinks and crimsons – in the ribs of harlequin beet, would for me, with fruit and fruit blossom, be more alluring to paint than a garden of flowers.

When I came to White Birch to do some more work, I was surprised, astonished even, by a new creature that was sitting, poised in the grass opposite the front door. It was bright pink with a lustrous finish. I had seen a version of it at Tate Modern in London, where it had attracted much attention, and I recognized it as Jeff Koons' *Balloon Dog*.

High yew hedges enclosed the space here, with a row of tall linden trees in front of the hedge on either side. The land sloped up to a grass terrace, where there was a seat backed by high, wide and rounded yew and boxwood, clipped to frame the seat; beyond was grass and a gap in the centre of the hedge, which let you through into the park, with its many fine oaks, beeches, maples and tulip trees, which beautifully furnished the space to the horizon and beyond.

There were two bare areas of grass either side of the site of *Balloon Dog*, which seemed to need something to occupy them – something green and simple, and nothing that would detract from the dog. So I suggested that Peter and Stephanie Brant's monogram should occupy these spaces, planted in boxwood, and with a wide box frame, scalloped on the inside, and spheres of box in each of the four corners.

I have still a design to carry out on the large lawn in front of the portico on the southern side of the main house, and there is already an idea floating about for that which I shall hope to pin down and realize in the not too distant future.

A view over crab apple blossom to the South Lawn and the woods

VILLA SALVIATI

MIGLIARINO, PISA

Il Duca and la Duchessa Salviati

My work on the garden surrounding the Villa Salviati at Migliarino, within a few miles of Pisa, which I was asked to design by the Duca and Duchessa Salviati in 2002, has not yet been entirely completed.

The villa, which was built in the mid-nineteenth century by Scipione Borghese, Duca Salviati, is of pale brick and stone, magnificent in its robust and bold architecture and fairly typical of the date, when taste was changing and ideas in architecture were moving away from the classical and the villa designs of the Renaissance. The land on which it stands was given to a member of the Salviati family at the end of the fifteenth century by the Republic of Florence, in gratitude for his collaboration, with Machiavelli and a scion of the Caffoni family, in the conquest of Pisa.

The mother of Scipione Borghese, the builder of Migliarino, was a Frenchwoman, Adèle de la Rochefoucauld. She was born in 1792 in a prison in Paris during the Revolution, and when she married Prince Borghese gave the name Borghese to the family's palazzo in Rome.

Scipione Borghese's wife was another Frenchwoman, Arabella Fitz-James, who was directly descended from James II and his mistress Arabella (or Arabelle) Churchill, whose children all bore the surname Fitz-James (meaning son of James). The descendants of their son James, Duke of Berwick and Marshal of France, became the French Ducs de Fitz-James (and also, in another line, the Spanish Dukes of Alba). It was Arabella Fitz-James who, as the Duchessa of Scipione Borghese, Duca Salviati, chose a French architect from Alsace, a M. Froelicher, to build their new house.

The building has an air of uncompromising solidity. You are met on the north side of the house by a balustraded perron, which curves down on either side of a central window to the ground below. This staircase leads up to a terrace, where lies the main entrance to the house, flanked by tall windows which look out on to a vista encompassing woods composed chiefly of oak, sweet chestnut and an immense forest of pines, which was planted by Scipione.

Pinus pinea, the umbrella or stone pine, was one growing there, a distinct tree with a flat-topped or umbrella-shaped head of spreading branches which has edible nuts. They are delicious cooked in the Migliarino way, first being scattered with salt and then toasted in a hot oven till brown and crisp. Small boys were employed to shin up the tall trees to pick or shake down the nuts, but today it is not easy to persuade boys to do such a job, their interests possibly being more sophisticated, and as a result the price of the nuts has rocketed. The other pine that grows here is the maritime pine, *P. pinaster*, a tall tree, sparsely branched with its bare trunk covered in a reddish brown or purple bark shaped into small squares. Both these pines revel in growing near the sea and in the sandy soil. *P. pinaster* is a source of turpentine and resin, and there is an industry in western France which supplies both in large quantities.

The Villa Salviati, in dappled sunlight

To return for a moment to the villa. This was surrounded by a sweep of gravel, all-encompassing and allowing no privacy on any side. This lack of privacy was the main problem I was asked to resolve. The family wanted a place where they could sit outside, with a measure of protection, not only from wind and weather but also from people and even cars, which would arrive at the front door and then drive away round the house.

I managed to devise a plan with a system of hedges planted with bay, *Laurus nobilis*, the laurel of antiquity, Petrarch's crown, whose dark green aromatic leaves are used for flavouring. It makes a good evergreen hedge and looks well when it is clipped. A strongly critical comment was made on my design by a child of the family who, when she saw the changes that had been made, burst into floods of tears and ran crying to her grandmother, complaining loudly, which only underlined what most of us know – how much children hate change. It was a discouraging comment, but in spite of this cry of protest, the grown-ups approved the plans. I also suggested an oval of grass in the gravel in front of the main door, so that cars could come and go without having to drive round the house, and also an area there, carved out of the ground beneath the trees, where cars could be parked.

There were two other difficulties which strongly affected planting plans, one major and one minor. Rabbits, pheasants and field mice were all serious predators on plants at Migliarino. Rabbits could be shot or netted and mice could be trapped, but none of these methods were totally successful in keeping the numbers down. And it was now illegal to shoot pheasants. So to a certain extent the pests had to be lived with. The minor discouragement was the soil, which was not far from being pure sand and therefore not the first choice of many plants and bulbs if they were to thrive.

As there was no formal garden round the house, the main area for planting was to be where there were sweeps of grass extending under trees and backed by the woodland. I managed to find a few places where some small ornamental shrubs and flowering plants could be planted near the house, and then I concentrated on the planting in the area of grass.

The spring was the season the Duchessa asked me to plant for especially, so, although limited by the nature of the soil, the choice of flowers and plants was a large one, For the first spring I planted narcissus in quantity, chiefly the small varieties, like N. 'Hawera', that naturalize well; *Crocus chrysanthus* and *C. tommasinianus*; species tulips, *T. batalinii* and *T. humilis*; grape hyacinths, scilla and chionodoxa, to make pools of blue; *Anemone blanda*, the blue shades and the one called 'White Splendour'; and *Ornithogalum nutans*, with its curly silvery-white green-striped flower heads, and *O. umbellatum*, the star of Bethlehem, which will spread quickly if it is content. *Puschkinia scilloides* var. *libanotica* was planted too, and for later in the year, August to October, *Sternbergia lutea*, which it is thought may have been the flower of the 'lilies of the field', for it grows widely in Palestine, Greece and Turkey.

Alas, alas! I had not made sufficient allowance for the depredations of the wildlife. The crocus and tulip bulbs were caviar to the pheasants, the rabbits relished mowing the tops off things, and the field mice, not being choosy, found that any bulb made a feast for them. All these pestilential beasts had a banquet. But although that first spring, eagerly looked forward to, was something of a flop, gallantly the Duchessa wanted to have another go. The narcissus had been a success, the sternbergias as well, along with several other bulbs, so the plantings had not been an entire disaster. Meanwhile, I had discovered that dipping bulbs in in a thick sauce of water and cayenne pepper (see page 124 for the recipe) had successfully deterred mice at my house in France, and I thought we should try it here too.

The autumn of 2006 saw the last planting of bulbs for the spring, and later the autumn ones will be planted. I suggested other flowers for spring which will flourish under a light canopy of trees, one being the sweet violet, *Viola odorata*, and its numerous cultivars. A dressing of leafmould will encourage it to spread and the scent on the air is delicious as you stroll through spring woods.

Now, as I write in December, the next spring is awaited with hope but nevertheless some anxiety. Will the mice and pheasants, and perhaps the rabbits, have been repelled by the pepper, or will they have found it only adds extra spice to their favourite dish?

WORLD YOUTH ALLIANCE GARDEN

NEW YORK

In 2005, I became involved in a project for creating a garden quite unlike anything I had done before. The garden was in New York at the back of a five-storey brownstone house. A space that, I learnt, is called in that city a yard.

My involvement stemmed from an interest I had in an organization called the World Youth Alliance. My attention had been drawn to it when I heard of a conference held in Vienna on 'Human Dignity and the Failure of Communism'. This conference was organized in November 2004 by the World Youth Alliance and the Neuwaldegg Institute and was to be addressed by key players in the downfall of Communism, such as Václav Havel, Archduke Otto von Habsburg and Wladyslaw Bartoszewski. I felt I would like to know more about the World Youth Alliance and talked to a Polish girl I knew who shared my interest, Emilia Klepacka (she is now, incidentally, Director of the World Youth Alliance Europe).

She contacted Anna Halpine, the President of the WYA, who came to see me and told me the story of the birth of the Alliance, and I will quote her words during an interview she gave. 'I was attending', she said, 'a United Nations conference in New York on population and development. The UN brought thirty-two young people into the conference to participate. But it quickly became apparent to the rest of us that the majority of UN-selected delegates were caught up in politically correct nostrums and not interested in engaging in basic issues confronting most the world's youth – issues such as potable water, human dignity, basic health care, education and human rights. I was with a handful of young people who felt the issues being discussed did not represent our concerns, so we went in the next day with a letter laying out an agenda addressing our concerns and presented it to the delegates. For two hours, the conference stalled, and in that time the world divided.

'The representatives of the developing nations struggling to free themselves from oppression, poverty and disease came to us one by one and said, "Thank you. Thank you for being here. Please come into our countries and work with our young people." And that really was the beginning of the World Youth Alliance.'

Anna Halpine was then twenty-two years of age and her colleague twenty-one. The Alliance was formed in 1999 and it now has over a million members from more than a hundred different nationalities, ethically, culturally and religiously diverse but united by their support for promoting the dignity of the person and the principles of the charter of the Alliance.

The yard garden of the headquarters of the World Youth Alliance in its first year – the planting still to be completed. To make as much as possible of the space, the main area is paved with limestone, and I designed the half-circular benches around the trees for seating. The narrow bed at the far end has room for bamboos, and later there will be climbers clothing the walls.

In 2004, I was in New York to give a lecture and to design the garden at White Birch Farm in Connecticut, which I write about on page 148. Anna came to breakfast with me. She looked so young and vulnerable, but I knew she was a tower of strength and determination, and that the smiling face, humour and gentle voice hid a heart that was loving but of steel. It was at the meal of porridge and eggs that she told me of the gift to the Alliance of a fine house in 72nd Street which was to be the headquarters of the Alliance in the USA and would also have rooms so students could stay there. She spoke of the area at the back of the house, which she had a vision of as a garden where parties could be held for members of the Alliance and which would provide a quiet oasis for students and workers staying in the house.

She asked if I would design this space and create a garden there. I had by then been asked to become a member of the international board of the Alliance and I felt there would be no better opportunity, or a more delightful one, to help in a small way an organization which I had come wholeheartedly to admire.

The area to be planned as a garden was not large, only 34 × 20 feet. There were high walls on three sides and five trees growing at the far end, which allowed little light and sun to fall into the space. So as to gain more, two of these trees were taken out, and the rough, drab-coloured plaster of the walls were washed with a not too deep ochre colour, a pattern of which I got from Provence, where it is found in the natural earths surrounding the small town of Roussillon. This treatment lightened up the yard a great deal, and when the sun was shining it fell through the branches and spaces of the three remaining trees.

There had to be space in the yard for people gathering there and benches so that they could sit and rest, so I paved the main area with limestone, and I designed half-circle benches to go round the three remaining trees as well as at the sides of the plot, with narrow borders behind them. Here there would be bamboos, and even though the more tender roses and plants such as trachelospermum and jasmines would not survive the hard New York winters, some tough climbing roses could be planted against the walls, along with spring, summer and autumn clematis, honeysuckle and other hardy climbers.

I looked for a way to introduce the sound of water and the note of freshness it could bring to the stifling heat of a New York summer, and considered a wall fountain, but finally introduced a group of three fine jets of different heights, which sprang from three small holes in the paving near a seat at the far end of the garden. The shade was light enough under the three trees to plant blue *Anemone blanda* and the one called 'White Splendour' as well as bulbs for spring and autumn. Crocus, scillas and some small tough narcissus would look well, too, with *Cyclamen coum* and lily of the valley for spring and *C. hederifolium* plus the autumn *Crocus speciosus* for autumn.

On 11 July 2006, the garden was opened with a party for all who had been involved in the re-creation of the interior and exterior of the house to make it fit for its intended purpose as the headquarters in the USA of the World Youth Alliance. The members of the board were there, and many of the young members working to support the Alliance, and it was an exciting moment to see the house and garden crowded with people pleased that it could at last be used. The disorder and chaos of the last months had transformed the place into an oasis of peace and calm. The air was warm and the sun shone.

I was very aware that the garden was still quite unfurnished. However, I reassured myself that it would in another year be full of greenery and colour. The bare arch and walls would be clothed by *Clematis montana* 'Elizabeth', deliciously scented climbing roses and honeysuckles. The early months, when the winter had passed, would see the spring flowering, and in the following months there would be the flowers of summer and early autumn. With the trees and bamboos, and pots planted with clipped box placed as I planned at the ends of each bench and in a few other spots, there should be a few green notes in the landscape even in winter.

It will make, I hope, a garden that will be a serene and peaceful place for the hard-working young people who gather there.

A TOWN GARDEN

A FANTASY GARDEN FOR
HOUSE & GARDEN

In 2000, I was asked to do something in the line of garden designing which was very different from anything I had done before. It came to me quite unexpectedly, in the form of a letter not from someone asking me to design a garden for them but from the magazine *House & Garden*. Tania Compton, the garden editor of the magazine, was planning to publish a series of articles featuring imaginary gardens, each dreamt up by a different garden designer, and she asked me if I would design and write about one of the gardens in the series.

I thought it would be fun. I agreed to do it and began to work on it at once. *House & Garden* ruled that it was to be an urban garden and they set out what its site, aspect and existing features were.

The house was a nineteenth-century one on four floors. Its south façade overlooked the back garden, which was 62 × 26 feet, with brick boundary walls, east and west, and a garage/shed at the northern rear boundary. There was interior access from a sunken basement or terrace overhead, with exterior access from a side passage and rear structure. A flowering cherry overhung the eastern side of the garden; various shrubs and a lawn comprised the central area, with a paved terrace in front of the northern structure. The neighbours' gardens either side were leafy, and there was a large magnolia tree to the west and a mature horse chestnut to the east.

Seven garden designers had been asked to suggest a scheme for this urban garden and their ideas for it were to be published each month for seven months.

Here is a character sketch I dreamt up of the fantasy couple and their garden. This London house has been bought by a couple in early middle age with grown-up children. Neither has had much interest in plants or gardens before. He is an historian and the author of several well-received books. She was involved in journalism and still writes occasional articles for newspapers and magazines on subjects of topical interest; she is writing her first novel. She is a good and interested cook. They have between them a considerable circle of friends. These are a catholic mixture and, as might be expected, largely drawn from the worlds of literature and journalism. They enjoy entertaining, and lunches or dinners for eight to ten guests are fairly frequent. In the summer, they want to be able to entertain larger numbers in the garden.

They are eager for their garden to have an unusual design – not be a run-of-the-mill London garden. It should have low maintenance costs, and be light on labour, as they do not fancy doing too much work in it. At the same time, they want it to be filled with colour and scent, at least in the spring and summer, and for it still to look interesting in the winter.

I suggested to them that a knot garden might give them all they wished and described to them the beauties and practicalities of knot gardens.

The garden will be beautiful in both spring and summer. In spring, bulbs, corms and tubers, with their vivid or pale-coloured flowers and fresh green leaves, will make the knot jewel-like. In summer, roses, lilies and abundant herbs and plants within the knot and in the surrounding borders will create a garden rich and lush in colour and foliage. In the winter, the green of the box, topiary, holly, bay laurel, olive tree and *Cupressus sempervirens*, the Italian cypress, will keep it loooking well furnished. Carefully planted pots will give extra colour and scent, and could have removable liners so that evergreens could be substituted for flowering plants in winter. A cobbled star, with stone bowl, water lily, fish and a simple jet of water, is set in the finest fawn-coloured Malvern gravel – York paving could be too dark and heavy-looking. The cobbles, in two colours, are small – for comfort underfoot – and edged with narrow, flat stones.

The shed at the end of the garden has two nicely framed windows. Two steps lead to the door, at the end of a cobbled path that incorporates a monogram of the owners' initials in darker cobbles. The door and windows are surrounded by climbers – one or two roses and a honeysuckle, perhaps *Lonicera periclymenum* 'Graham Thomas', which flowers long and abundantly and is especially scented.

The shed could be adapted as a 'cottage' for writing and reading when the weather is chilly. When the sun comes out, bringing warmer days, the owners can sit out, even eat out, and lie in long chairs to nap or to read. For their summer parties, they will be able to gather in the space in front of the 'cottage' and around the fountain.

Two bench seats made from slatted wood and furnished with cushions are attached to the west and east walls by hinges, supported by movable stays so they can be let down to hang flat against the wall to save space.

I have chosen plants that will harmonize and look at home in and around a knot garden. Mostly these are plants that were popular in the sixteenth and seventeenth centuries, the heyday of the knot garden. Quite a few of them have evergreen or grey foliage, which will help the garden to look furnished in winter. There will be plenty of herbs for cooking.

A once-yearly clipping of the box hedges in June should be sufficient to keep them tidy. For the hedges, plants between 8 to 10 inches high should be chosen and planted the same distance apart as their height. To maintain this garden in good order would take about three or four hours a week – a little more perhaps when the hedges are being clipped and when the climbers and roses have to be pruned, and at other times a little less.

What fun it would be for me if one day a real-life literary couple with an urban house stumbled on this design and were able to fit it into their back garden – perhaps to spend many happy hours there.

Plants for the borders and knots

TREES
Cupressus sempervirens
Ilex aquifolium 'Argentea Marginata'
Laurus nobilis
Olea europaea

BOX HEDGES
Buxus sempervirens

CLIMBERS
Clematis flammula
Jasminum officinale
Lonicera periclymenum
Periploca graeca

ROSES
Rosa × alba
Rosa ardencies
Rosa arvensis
Rosa 'Burgundiaca'
Rosa × centifolia
Rosa 'De Meaux'
Rosa 'De Resht'
Rosa gallica 'Versicolor'
Rosa × gallica var. *officinalis*
Rosa mascara
Rosa rubiginosa

SHRUBS
Artemisia abrotanum
Ballota pseudodictamnus
Hyssopus officinalis
Lavandula angustifolia
Rosmarinus officinalis
Ruta graveolens
Santolina chamaecyparissus

SUB-SHRUBS/PERENNIALS
Aquilegia vulgaris
Armeria maritima
Bellis perennis
Calamintha cretica
Calamintha grandiflora
Chrysanthemum balsamita
Clematis recta

Corydalis ochroleuca
Dianthus caryophyllus
Dianthus plumarius
Dictamnus albus
Dictamnus albus var. *purpureus*
Doronicum × *excelsum*
Eryngium alpinum
Euphorbia myrsinites
Geranium macrorrhizum
Helleborus niger
Hesperis matronalis var. *albiflora*
Lathyrus vernus
Melissa officinalis
Origanum vulgare
Paradisea liliastrum
Primula auricula
Primula veris
Primula vulgaris
Ranunculus aconitifolius 'Flore Pleno'
Ranunculus asiaticus
Saponaria officinalis
Satureja montana
Saxifraga rotundifolia
Thymus serpyllum
Thymus vulgaris
Viola odorata
Viola tricolor
BULBS, TUBERS AND CORMS
* = Bulbs requiring full sun
Allium moly
Anemone coronaria
Anemone hortensis
Crocus aureus
Crocus biflorus
Crocus nudiflorus
Crocus sativus
Crocus susianus
Cyclamen coum
Cyclamen purpurascens
Cyclamen repandum
Erythronium dens-canis

Fritillaria imperialis *
Fritillaria latifolia *
Fritillaria nigra *
Fritillaria persica *
Galanthus nivalis
Gladiolus communis subsp. *byzantinus* *
Hermodactylus tuberosus *
Hyacinthus italicus
Hyacinthus orientalis *
Iris 'Fiorentina' *
Iris graminea *
Iris latifolia *
Iris pumila *
Iris xiphium *
Leucojum aestivum
Leucojum vernum
Lilium bulbiferum var. *croceum*
Lilium candidum *
Lilium chalcedonicum *
Lilium martagon
Lilium pyrenaicum
Muscari azureum
Muscari botryoides
Muscari comosum
Narcissus bulbocodium
Narcissus florepleno
Narcissus jonquilla
Narcissus × *odorus*
Narcissus triandrus
Narcissus viridiflorus*
Ranunculus lingua 'Grandiflorus' (water plant) *
Romulea columnae *
Scilla bifolia
Scilla italica
Scilla liliohyacinthus
Scilla peruviana *
Scilla peruviana 'Alba' *
Sternbergia lutea
Tulipa acuminata *
Tulipa clusiana *
Zephyranthes atamasca *

SYON HOUSE

MIDDLESEX

The Duke and Duchess of Northumberland

Hardly ten miles from London stands Syon, which is the only part of the tidal River Thames with water meadows and a natural foreshore. The site and the house have a long and eventful history. It may have been near Syon that the Romans crossed the Thames in 54 BC, and later there were Roman and Saxon settlements at nearby Brentford, where in 1016 the Saxon King Edmond Ironside defeated the Danes, led by Canute. A religious house founded by Henry V in 1415, fulfilling his father's penance for the part he played in the death of Richard II, was constructed on the present site of Syon House. It was occupied by the Brigettine Order, founded in the fourteenth century by St Bridget, a Swedish mystic. The abbey took its name from Mount Zion in the Holy Land and Syon (Sion) is named after the abbey.

The foundations of similar Brigettine abbeys show them based on an inner cloister for nuns and an outer one for priests, deacons and lay brothers. It is thought that the central courtyard of Syon House may have been part of the nuns' cloister. And archaeological work carried out recently by London University has revealed the foundations of an enormous church, extending almost from a ha-ha between the house and the river, right under the house and the courtyard.

This is an especially interesting thought for me, as in 1998 I was asked by the Duke and Duchess of Northumberland if I would design a garden for this courtyard. I already knew the house well, and had many times thought to myself how pretty the courtyard could be made – changed from a rather sombre, sad place to something that could be looked down on from the windows of the house and walked in with pleasure. I looked at some drawings showing the house and the courtyard as they were in 1632: at this time, the courtyard was simply planted with grass from wall to wall. In another drawing showing how it looked in 1847, there were what appear to be shrubs planted at the base of all the walls, but of course this may only have been artist's licence. In 1761 Robert Adam, who had designed the main rooms of the house, proposed a rotunda for the courtyard, which, beautiful though it no doubt would have been, would surely have kept out light from every window.

I seem to remember that there were some plants in the courtyard when I first saw it, but I cannot at all recall what they were. In later years it had a beautifully modelled lead fox, sitting on a robust stone plinth placed there by the 10th Duke, who was the Master of the Percy hounds and a keen fox-hunting man. This did nothing for itself or for the courtyard it sat in, and the present Duke and Duchess were happy to move it. It went to Alnwick, where it looks well in the centre of a circle where various paths conjoin in the new garden there, suitably in the heart of the Percy hunting country.

Now there was a relatively clear space where I could concentrate on creating a design which I hoped would not only be a pleasure to contemplate from the windows of the rooms that looked down on it,

The central courtyard garden of Syon House. I designed a simple parterre of curved box-edged beds surrounding a central pool and fountain. Pale cream and white flowers and foliage in light green and silver brighten the shade.

but would be practical to use during the dinners, weddings and other events which at certain times of year take place at Syon. So the considerations was not purely aesthetic. I had to create a design that allowed for a large number of people to move comfortably around the garden.

Surprisingly, although the court is totally enclosed by the four walls of the house, which were many feet high, it can be extremely windy within it, so this was something else that had to be considered. The windows looking into the court are undecorated by any sort of architrave, pediment or moulded surround – which gives them a curiously unfinished look – although a 1632 drawing shows pointed architraves above the windows.

I thought a movement of water would add sparkle and sound and bring life to a space which could be somewhat shady and overcast, and I drew two different designs for the garden, both using water. Each had a circular fountain in the centre of the design, with a stone surround encircled by a low hedge of box (*Buxus sempervirens*), but plan number two had four other fountains, each a narrow oval with pointed ends, also stone edged with, again, low box hedges surrounding them. Each fountain had a single simple jet of water. Plan number one had eight beds of flowers in the corners of the court around

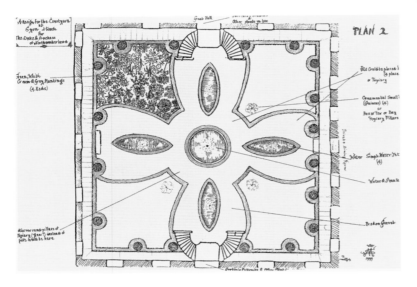

a central seat backed by box to be clipped into billowing rounds like pillows at the back of the seats, with four flower beds curved around the central fountain. All the beds would be enclosed with box hedges, but before the box was planted, a wooden edging would be fixed round them, six inches high, enabling the beds to be slightly raised above the paths, which would be covered in a fine Breedon gravel in a pale beige colour. The beds would be planted with flowers and bulbs in whites and creams with grey and silver foliage plants such at *Helichrysum italicum* and artemisias.

On the east and west there were staircases leading one from the great hall, the other from the dining room (what the French call a perron) curving elegantly down into the court. At the top of these staircases, there was a space and here I suggested containers should be placed, and planted with scented flowers such as Surfinia petunias, silver-leaved *Helichrysum petiolare* 'Blue Vein', white scented violas and other annual scented plants in white or cream. I felt that to keep the garden looking light and to help mitigate the rather sombre light in the courtyard it would be better to have a largely white, green and cream palette of colour and so suggested silvers and greys, aquilegias, foxgloves, phlox, lupins and thymes as well as many lilies, from the early-flowering *Lilium regale* to late-flowering Asiatic lilies, tulips, scillas, *Hydrangea arborescens* 'Annabelle', pansies and violas, oriental poppies, nicotiana, dictamnus, penstemons, anthemis, nigella and *Chrysanthemum parthenium*, as well as a lavatera, all in their white-flowered varieties, plus a white-flowered lavender and rosemary. Stone seats would be placed here and there in both plans, and also pale terracotta pots filled with white-flowered scented geraniums near the seats, with clipped box topiaries when the weather was too cold for tender things. The box could be grown in metal liners with drainage holes which could easily be dropped into the terracotta pots in the winter.

The Duke and Duchess chose plan number one and work started. First, a soil test was carried out and the soil was found to be slightly acid and generally satisfactory for the growth of plants; but the principal factors affecting plant growth here were likely to be shade, eddying winds and rain shadow.

Before the real work of creating the garden could begin, there were two or three possible difficulties to be explored and, I hoped, overcome. One was to discover if the broad band of paving which ran round the court at the foot of the house walls could be lifted in places to allow the planting of cypresses between each of the windows, as well as some climbing roses.

A second query that had to be answered was how was the water to reach the central fountain. Mercifully, all the services for Syon House run below the basement, so to run water into the courtyard would be relatively straightforward. The paving slabs were a different kettle of fish. They served an

important purpose, in that they shed water from the walls of the house and also covered the foundations, to plant into which would not have made any tree or rose very happy. Therefore, the planting area was brought forward and good soil and well-rotted manure were introduced into the excavated holes. Naturally a certain amount of room in the court was lost, but not enough to affect the design.

At last these few difficulties were overcome and work began, continuing throughout March, April and May. Paying frequent visits to the site over these months, I was much impressed by the enthusiasm, hard work and dedication shown by all involved, led by the head gardener, Mr Topher Martyn, who had been in on the project from the beginning and had been a great help to me.

There was a deadline to be met. The garden had to be finished for an event on the evening of 9 June and this was to be an important one, for HRH The Prince of Wales was to come to it and the garden would be seen for the first time, illuminated by its new lighting.

The deadline was met and during the evening, His Royal Highness was given a tour of this small court. He pronounced himself pleased with what he saw.

Above The perron from the house to the courtyard, planted, as is the garden, only with white-flowered plants **Opposite** Alternative plans for the courtyard. The Duke and Duchess chose the top one.

CROSBY HALL

LONDON

Christopher Moran

If you are walking or driving along the Embankment in London or crossing Battersea Bridge in a northerly direction, your eye may be arrested by a rare sight in this city, and an especially rare one amongst the twentieth-century architecture that litters the far bank of the River Thames. How strange and mysterious to see a Tudor palace in such a setting!

On closer inspection, it can be recognized as a new building. Its soft red brick and pale stone, its oriel window, elaborately carved ornamentation, heraldic devices and lions perched on a pair of columns either side of a massive oak door have quite taken you in. It's as though a piece of Hampton Court Palace, with all the flamboyance of Tudor architectural fashion and rich decorations, had made a mysterious arrival in twenty-first-century London. There is even a hexagonal bell tower rising behind the oriel window's gable, topped by a gilded weather vane, its roof adorned with fishscale tiles. Two other vanes on two other towers, of differing design, rise from behind the façade, and they too are gilded; if it is a sunny day, the light meeting these touches of gold brings an extra sparkle and glamour to the whole building.

The history of the creation of this twenty-first-century palace is a gripping tale involving England's most remarkable and enigmatic figure, Sir Thomas More. A knight is in the story as well; silks from Italy and the East, kings, the Wars of the Roses, Edward IV, Richard III and William Shakespeare.

It starts in the year 1452. Sir John Crosby was a rich merchant, trading in textiles, notably silk. He was a freeman of the Grocers' Company. Knighted in 1471 by Edward IV for his support of the White Rose of York, he was also a soldier, a diplomat and politician. He had built, near St Helen's in Bishopsgate in the City of London, a house which was clearly a notable one in its time. Taking nine years to build, it was described as being both 'large and beautiful, and the highest in London'. This palace, for that was what it must have been, included a Great Hall, and during the sixteenth century the whole set of buildings was lived in by a succession of powerful men: the Duke of Gloucester, later Richard III (Shakespeare wrote about Crosby Hall in his play about that time), merchants and statesmen, foreign bigwigs – and that man of singular virtue, Sir Thomas More, saint and martyr.

In the seventeenth and eighteenth centuries, Sir John's remarkable house did not fare well, but as Dr Simon Thurley has written, it has always been 'recognised by architects and antiquarians as one of the most precious survivals on the square mile'. In 1908, its then owner, the Chartered Bank, demolished the remaining parts of the building and in 1910 re-sited the Great Hall, moving it stone by stone to Chelsea, appropriately into part of the garden of Sir Thomas More's Chelsea house, now Cheyne Walk. In 1926, in an attempt to find an appropriate use for the hall, several schemes were tried. None was successful and the British Federation of University Women, who employed the architect Walter Godfrey to build, at right angles to the hall, a residential block in the Arts and Crafts manner, finally took it over on a long lease. Later, in the 1950s and early 1960s, more buildings were added by the architects Cordan and Godfrey, and from 1926 to 1992, Crosby Hall was the hall of residence for the women students and graduates. The Greater London Council were the freeholders of the hall and after this body's abolition in 1988, and the hall's vacating by the British Federation of University Women, it was bought by Mr Christopher Moran.

Mr Moran is a businessman who had made a study in depth of the art and architecture of the sixteenth century and built up a considerable collection of Tudor furniture and pictures. He had been interested in the Hall since the 1970s and now, having decided this was to be his home and that of his collection, he demolished what he could of the 1950s and 1960s buildings. The residential block, however, was a listed building, so demolition was unlikely to be an option, and he decided to adapt it

The main entrance from the Embankment into the courtyard garden and the stairs to the terrace. Narrow knots with mop-headed holly standards – both green and variegated – line the Portland stone path, and mounds of gilded rosemary mark the foot of the stone staircase.

to look Jacobean. He called in scholars including Dr Thurley, for several years Curator of the Royal Palaces, and then Curator of the Museum of London, to help him design, to his own specifications, the buildings he wanted to create in sympathy with Sir John Crosby's Great Hall and which were to form a quadrangle which, it was hoped, would put the Hall back into its proper context.

There was not enough evidence to copy Sir John Crosby's house, and anyway the site at Chelsea was quite different from the one at Bishopsgate, so it was decided, and here I quote Dr Thurley, 'to create a new house that would give the illusion of having been built over a period of 150 years and thus a setting for the old Hall that could have really existed. Modern building techniques were to be used but every detail, form and feature was to be based on an identifiable precedent from the sixteenth century.' This meant that each range was based on a specific building, and its detailing was taken from either that or a contemporary building. Architectural display in the sixteenth century was dominated by heraldic motives and badges; faithful to this convention, Mr Moran had the College of Arms devise for him a coat of arms that could be adapted to adorn the building.

The quadrangle consists of four ranges. The east range incorporates Crosby Great Hall and is in Danvers Street. The entrance range is based on Cardinal Wolsey's 1520s base court at Hampton Court Palace; its loggia follows those at Horton Court, Gloucestershire, and a later house, Dingley Hall, Northamptonshire. The gateway into Cheyne Walk takes its inspiration from the oriel window at Hengrave Hall and the pillars of Henry VIII's vanished palace at Rochester. Dr Thurley again: 'the intention of this range is to capture the heraldic flamboyance of Henry VIII's reign, and the charming mix of late-Gothic and Renaissance details that characterises the first half of the sixteenth century.' The dining-hall range on the east, modelled closely on that of Kirby Hall in Northamptonshire, is made entirely in stone, its frieze incorporating Mr Moran's heraldic badges of sea stags and stars. 'It takes the story of English architecture up to the 1570s and expresses the mannerism that characterised many houses belonging to Elizabethan courtiers.'

The great door of the north range is closely modelled on one in the South Court at Hatfield House, and the clever remodelling of Godfrey's Arts and Crafts wing has created an elevation characteristic of around 1600. The lower two floors have been made into one creation, a double-height entrance hall with magnificent plasterwork, ceiling and frieze, and an elaborate marble chimneypiece. The tall gables of this range remind one of Chastleton in Oxfordshire. The coat of arms, and the strapwork creating winged victories, have been carved in stone by Dick Reid of York and the windows in the Great Hall are gradually being filled with painted glass based on the engravings of the Flemish designer Hans Vredaman.

Sir John Crosby's hall on the east range has a wonderful interior with an oak scissor roof, the first of its kind. From the meeting point of the arches of the ceiling hang pendants ending in octagonal ornaments pierced with small niches. Each pendant forms the centre of four arches of elegant construction while the spandrels are pierced with perpendicular trefoil-headed niches. The oriel window is vaulted with stone and beautifully groined; the ribs spring from small pillars attached to the angles with knots of foliage and bosses at the points of intersection. In the centre is the ram trippant, the crest of Sir John Crosby. The door architraves, the fireplace and the window surrounds are all of the original Reigate stone.

The state of the outside walls of the hall itself caused some discussion because when it was moved to Chelsea it had been faced in Portland stone and so lost much of its fifteenth-century character. After a certain amount of debate, it was decided to create a stone balustrade bearing Mr Moran's motto, not unlike one at Rushden, Northamptonshire.

The palace is a beautiful creation which in one building tells the story of English architecture and craftsmanship from the second half of the sixteenth century to the early seventeenth century, and it is a heart-lifting experience to look at the exquisite work and to realize that in the twenty-first century there are craftsmen who have the same skills as those possessed by their ancestors who were living nearly five hundred years ago.

It is about here that I come into the story. Mr Moran asked me whether I would design a garden for the courtyard of Crosby Hall. As a gardener who has lived the greater part of her life in Tudor, Elizabethan and Stuart houses and designed gardens for them, perhaps a few more than for those which surround houses of a later period, to be asked to design a garden for this Elizabethan palace promised to be an enjoyable challenge.

There was little need to have much discussion

Looking over the flower-filled knot to the sixteenth-century Great Hall of Sir John Crosby's palace

about what shape this garden would take, nor about what plants would go into it. Mr Moran did not want any plants that were not of the period, and I was happy with this, for I felt that if any so-called 'exotics' crept in, they might not be in harmony with the architecture of the palace. The garden would be furnished only with the plants grown in the knot gardens of the period and those introduced into Britain by John Tradescant and his son who, as the sixteenth and early seventeenth centuries' most famous plant hunters and gardeners, travelled far and wide in Europe and the New World. The archives at Hatfield hold some of Tradescant's bills and the lists of plants bought, or found, on his plant-hunting expeditions for his patron, Robert Cecil, the 1st Earl of Salisbury. I knew these well from past work.

So there was a good guide and precedent for what the character of the courtyard garden at Crosby Hall should be, and for the plants that would fill it – although I hoped it would also have a character and originality of its own. I set about drawing a design for the enclosed space of the courtyard.

There was to be a fountain too, commissioned by Mr Moran and dedicated to Diana, the goddess of hunting. The figure was skilfully carved by the sculptor Nell Simmons and the upper and lower basins were made from English Derbyshire limestone and Cumberland slate. In Tudor gardens the centrepiece, and that for the courtyards of palaces, was essentially an elaborate fountain and Mr Moran chose to have his modelled on one that had been in the gardens of Nonsuch Palace. John, Lord Lumley, had installed it there sometime between 1579 and 1591 after visiting gardens in Italy, which had strongly influenced his garden designs.

There was more than one hiccough that threatened to upset the smooth progress of the garden plans. One of the most tricky was the result of an underground car park being made: a huge hump that appeared under the south end of the terrace wall. I contemplated it in some horror, wondering how that could be fitted into the vision of how I had thought the courtyard might ideally look. Mercifully

Two square flower-filled knots lie on either side of the fountain, which is modelled on one that had been at Nonsuch Palace in the late sixteenth century.

one day it had gone, although the car park had not. I never fathomed the mystery of how this had been achieved.

Luckily, having designed and planted several knots, I had in my head a list of the plants, bulbs and fruits of the Tudor period that could be planted here, and set to work to track them down. There was not going to be a great deal of room. There would be two square knots and some long, necessarily narrowish beds on either side of a central path laid with pale setts of Portland stone that led from the magnificent oak entrance gate to the main door that takes you through into the Great Hall. All these beds would be edged in box (*Buxus sempervirens*), as would the knotted patterns of the square beds and the divisions of the long beds.

In these last, I planted small standard mop-headed hollies, half plain dark green *Ilex aquifolium* and half *I.a.* 'Aurea Marginata', a variegated holly much used by the Tudors. The Elizabethans loved eccentric plants, those that did not conform to the normal in the plant world, and they collected for their gardens the variegated, the striped, the spotted and the double, whenever and wherever they could find them. They planted the great rose plantain, hose-in-hose primroses, the double ones as well, plus galligaskins, Jacks-in-the-green and Jacks-in-the-pulpit, which last have a Tudor ruff of coloured leaves beneath the bloom; auriculas, too: these had been had been brought to England from the Alps. How undaunted and adventurous they were, when you think how they had none of the facilities and aids to travel that modern-day plant hunters have! Mercifully all these plants could still be found, along with other suitable species, including bulbs and tubers.

With space restricted, it was essential to choose them especially carefully and to try to introduce colour for at least the months of spring and summer. For the very early part of the year, and autumn, it would be hard to find enough room for all the plants and bulbs. But the terrace could come in here and be used for planting, in copies of Elizabethan lead and terracotta pots, such plants as oleanders (introduced by Tradescant), orange, lemon and bay trees. For very early in the year, the containers could have spring bulbs, dog's-tooth violets, snowdrops and jonquils. There must be room for some herbs, such as thyme, marjoram and mint; rue, too, of course, and some medicinal herbs as well.

There were many roses of the right date. The white rose of York, *Rosa × alba* 'Alba Maxima' and the Red Rose of Lancaster (probably *R. gallica* var. *officinalis*) and, of course, Fair Rosamund's rose, Rosa Mundi (*R. gallica* 'Versicolor'), rose of the world, named after Henry II's mistress. *Rosa* 'Burgundiaca', with its tiny leaves and flowers, is the perfect size for one of the small spaces in a knot. I fitted in as many other Tudor roses as was possible, but space had to be left for plants that would give colour at the other seasons of the year and the only one of the ancient roses that flowered more than once was *R.* 'De

Resht', brought from Persia by Nancy Lindsay in the 1930s, producing its beautiful red flowers as late as November.

Into the knots went the doubles and eccentrics of the primrose tribe, plus auriculas, scillas, dog's-tooth violets and *Narcissus jonquilla*, the tender *N. tazetta*, and *N. poeticus*, all three exquisitely scented. There was one more narcissus to be found and planted here, N. 'Eystettensis', which surely must have been grown in the gardens of the Prince Bishop of Eystellant, who had all the plants in his gardens painted by Besler in 1612.

Another of the hiccoughs I mentioned earlier was the problem of shallowness of the soil. This did not matter as far as the knots were concerned, because they could be treated like raised beds and the soil could rise higher by several inches within the box hedges, but it did matter when you wanted to plant a tree such as an olive, as I planned to do, and some climbing roses. You could not go as deep as you wanted because the depth was limited by what went on beneath the 'floor', as it were, of the courtyard. The only thing to be done was to go as deep as possible (scarcely more than eighteen inches) and then, as far as the olive tree went, plant it on a low mound, while the roses had to take their chance with surface mulches and a raised patch of soil. I planted *Rosa moschata* and the Persian musk rose, *R.m. nasturana*, an early and a later flowerer, both beautifully scented and known to have flourished in Tudor gardens. There were very few wall spaces for climbing plants, but I planted a honeysuckle (*Lonicera periclymenum*) and a jasmine (*J. officinale*, introduced in 1528) on the stone banisters either side of the steps leading to the terrace, and a gilded rosemary, a plant much admired by the Elizabethan gardener, at the foot of each banister.

In the lawn grass around the olive tree, I planted *Crocus biflorus*, the Scottish crocus, much planted in the gardens of the time.

The olive is flourishing. It faces south in a warm sheltered corner. There is one in the Chelsea Physic Garden (in striking distance of Crosby Hall), which was planted in the seventeenth century and has been known to fruit, the rumour being that it has provided olives for the Curator's annual cocktail party. I much hope that with luck, sun and good management, this tree will do the same for the owner of Crosby Hall.

The apricot against the terrace wall produced fruit the first year it was planted and this year, a year later, it produced thirty-six plump and glowing apricots, enough for the dessert course of a banquet; and remember too there is little more beautiful in the month of March than the blossom on an apricot tree.

THE MUSEUM OF GARDEN HISTORY

LONDON

Along the banks of the River Thames at Lambeth, there are some strange, even grotesque, buildings, some towering upwards, some stretched out in block-like structures, one looking as though carved out of a monstrous green and yellow cheese, and then you see two buildings in extraordinary contrast to these manifestations of modern architecture, none of which has any coherent relation to each other.

These buildings are the Tudor gateway, built in a rose-red brick, which leads into Lambeth Palace, home to the Archbishop of Canterbury, its great oak door set in a central arch and entirely filling it. Alongside this gateway to Lambeth Palace lies a church, which was much altered in the eighteenth and nineteenth centuries, but which has a long history. Founded in AD 800, it is the resting place of five Archbishops of Canterbury, and it has a chapel of the Dukes of Norfolk and, within its churchyard, the tomb of a sailor who, famous in his time, is not forgotten today and whose name, Captain Bligh of the *Bounty*, conjures up pictures of mutiny on the high seas. He is in company with two bold and adventurous spirits who are still in our time admired, remembered and written about, and whose fine carved tomb lies near his. The tomb is that of the famous plant hunters the John Tradescants, father and son.

St Mary's at Lambeth, for that was the name of the church that lay alongside Lambeth Palace, its fourteenth-century tower a landmark on the river, was the Tradescants' parish church, where the family worshipped, and their house was near by, as well as their nursery garden where they grew the rare plants they brought back from their travels, and where they housed their collection of curiosities and rarities in a building called the Ark. A contemporary wrote that the Tradescants' Ark was a place where 'a man might in one daye, behold and collecte into one place more curiosities that hee should see if he spent all his life in travel'. In creating the Ark, the Tradescants had founded one of the world's first museums.

The younger Tradescant was a plant hunter like his father and quite as adventurous, three times sailing to Virginia in 1637, 1642 and 1654 and bringing back many plants and trees never before seen in the Old World, including one which took his name – *Tradescantia virginiana*.

Not long after the Second World War, the church was abandoned as the parish church of Lambeth and deconsecrated, the Church Commissioners having decided to sell the building and its site for development. It was an extraordinary decision and it looked as though the church was doomed. Then in the early 1970s, a wonderful thing happened: two more heroic figures arrived on the scene to take their place in the history of the church. They were John and Rosemary Nicholson. They both had a great interest in the early plant hunters and decided to visit the tomb of the Tradescants at St Mary's. They

A stone seat in a quiet corner of the knot garden

were horrified by what they saw in the graveyard surrounding the tomb. The scene was one of decay and desolation, a haunt for vagabonds and a sleeping place for tramps, scattered with litter and rubbish. They were equally shocked by the condition of the church inside, with its blackened walls and pillars, its monuments and windows suffering from neglect and as desolate as its exterior. But under all the dust and in spite of the gloomy atmosphere pervading it within and without, the building made a great impression on them, and they were dismayed when they heard of the demolition order that had been served on St Mary's and of the determination of the Church Commissioners to pull it down. On hearing the news, the Nicholsons made up their minds, there and then, that they would save it.

And so they did. Both the Nicholsons were courageous fighters, intelligent and resourceful, and forthwith they formed the Tradescant Trust to restore the building, and to found within it, the first

The tomb of the Tradescants

Museum of Garden History in the world. It was a very considerable achievement. Queen Elizabeth The Queen Mother gave her enthusiastic support and encouragement to the venture, and Her Majesty's continuing interest in the development of the museum was a great source of pride; when setbacks and disappointments occurred, of which there were not a few, her approval and help enabled all working for the Trust not to lose heart.

In 1977, I became involved in the trust, becoming its president, and later was asked by the trust's chairman, Mrs Nicholson, and the trustees, to design, lay out and plant, in the churchyard, a memorial garden to the Tradescants.

Steeped in the history of the plant hunters, Mrs Nicholson well knew my particular link with John Tradescant the Elder. I had been living at Hatfield House in Hertfordshire since 1972, where Tradescant had been head gardener to Robert Cecil, 1st Earl of Salisbury, my husband's ancestor. Tradescant's lists of plants bought for Hatfield, along with his bills and the evidence of his travels in

Spain, France, Italy, Russia and even to the Barbary coast in north Africa – ostensibly to fight the Barbary pirates but for Tradescant an opportunity to collect unusual plants, the apricot being one of the trees he brought back to Hatfield – were all to be found in the archives there, along with books of the sixteenth and seventeenth centuries describing gardens of that age, as well as illustrations of their designs.

After some study of the books and papers, I drew up a plan for the area, which was not large but presented considerable difficulties, the worst being the graves, many laid flat on the ground, making the laying of the paths a big headache. It was here that a member of the trust, John Drake, who was not only an architect but a gardener too, brought his skill and knowledge to help me in the laying out the space. One thing was certain: a memorial garden for the Tradescants to hold plants of the seventeenth century had to be a formal one, with, at its heart, a knot, a garden design used at both Hatfield and Cranborne by John the Elder. (For a description of the making and use of knot gardens see the chapter on Hatfield, pages 81–6.)

The knot garden at the museum I planned to fill with plants, bulbs and tubers grown by John Tradescant, and those brought from Virginia by his son on the three voyages he made there in the seventeenth century. These would be of interest for every season, starting with snowdrops, crocus, hepaticas and narcissus, through to scillas, tulips and *Fritillaria imperialis*, sixteenth- and seventeenth-century roses, martagon and Madonna lilies, and of course herbs; there would also be the cyclamen and the double and hose-in-hose primroses and cowslips grown by Tradescant. The knot was to be outlined in common box (*Buxus sempervirens*) and, to mark the Tradescants, the initial T on each side planted in silvery grey santolina(*Santolina chamaecyparissus*). There was not room for all the plants and trees I would have liked to plant, most of all a tulip tree (*Liriodendron tulipifera*), which had been brought from the New World by John the Younger. But we managed to plant an *Arbutus unedo*, the strawberry tree, with its creamy white flowers and red fruits, as well as a *Phillyrea latifolia*, much used for hedges by the Elizabethans. Against the east wall of the museum, where we put a seat, an early rose, *Rosa moschata*, was planted, with a hedge of sweetbrier (*R. rubiginosa*) on either side of the short path leading to it and a pair of crape myrtle bushes (*Myrtus communis*) embracing the seat. In the beds behind the sweetbrier hedge there was room for more plants of the period. Because there was a right of way through the churchyard, I planted a yew hedge (*Taxus baccata*) to protect and surrround the garden and give greater privacy for the museums' visitors.

The great wall of Lambeth Palace rears up behind a broad border facing south, planted with trees and shrubs of the period. The wall of the church is on the west, with lower walls on the east, which also seal the southern end of the garden. To have the sound of water in the garden, I found a stone wall fountain in Italy and a path leads to where it is mounted on the east wall. So that some of the many visitors can rest, stone benches, also from Italy, were placed in strategic positions here and there.

A necessity was a compost heap, and this was hidden away in a corner. It provided a most valuable mulch for the plants, along with manure, which the London Mounted Police used, in the early days, to provide. When Robert Runcie became Archbishop of Canterbury, elevated from the see of St Albans, the diocese in which we lived at Hatfield, I had great hopes that the charming little Tamworth pigs he kept there might be brought to Lambeth Palace, and had visions of all my manure problems being solved: a rope, a basket and over the neighbour's wall it would come – quantities of excellent farmyard manure! Alas, alack – no such luck! The Archbishop decided not to move his pigs – but he came to bless the garden in a solemn ceremony, and his then chaplain, who accompanied him, Richard Chartres, is now the Bishop of London.

The final seal on the garden came in 1978 when Her Majesty Queen Elizabeth The Queen Mother formally opened it, using, to cut the tape, a pair of seventeenth-century scissors loaned, by permission of Sir Roy Strong, from the Victoria and Albert Museum where he was then the Director.

As we pause to look at the great stone tomb of the Tradescants, standing in the garden planted with the flowers and trees they had collected on their many adventurous and hazardous travels, we read these lines:

Know, stranger, ere thou pass, beneath this stone
Lye John Tradescant grandsire, father, son
The last dy'd in his spring, the other two
Liv'd till they had travell'd Orb and Nature through,
By their choice Collections may appear,
Of what is rare, in land, in sea, in air
Whilst they (as Homer's Iliad in a nut)
A world of wonders in one closet shut
These famous Antiquarians that had been,
Both gardiners to the Rose and Lily Queen,
Transplanted now themselves, sleep here & when
Angels shall with their trumpets waken men,
And fire shall purge the world, these three shall rise
And change this Garden for Paradise.

And when those who come to visit the museum walk in its garden dedicated to the Tradescants, perhaps they may feel they are walking in another paradise, albeit an earthly one.

The knot garden, with the elegant lines of the box hedge marking an intricate Tudor design, and the initial letter of the Tradescants' name formed in silver-grey *Santolina chamaecyparissus*

A ROOF GARDEN IN CHELSEA

LONDON

The Dowager Marchioness of Salisbury

The Potting Bench

I find it astonishing to be writing about a roof garden and even more astonishing that it should be my own roof garden. I had never in my life before lived in London, and it had not occurred to me that I ever would.

I had vivid memories of brief stays there when I was seven and my elder sister eight, and they are almost all disagreeable ones, the only exception being that of a ride in the open top of a double-decker bus. I remember visits to the dentist, and being dressed up in smart clothes to walk with our governess in the park – hated hats, coats and gloves, and worst of all, gaiters, with multiple buttons that had to be done up with a button hook. No stuffing indoors was allowed, so we played on what were called, in my grandparents' house, 'the leads', and took our dolls there, heaping soot and town dust as an alternative to making pies with healthy country mud.

At night, fire engines, bells ringing (there must have been a fire station close by) rushed past the house, terrifying my sister and me; we were convinced we were going to be burnt to death, and we used to climb out of our beds and sniff around the passages to see if we could smell burning. As with all small children, it never crossed our minds to tell the grown-ups of our fears. These memories cast a gloom over the thought of ever living in London.

Later on there were happy memories, but they were quite different – London in the war, in the Blitz, searchlights raking the sky, but great fun and happiness, jazz and dancing and the milk train back to base – the military hospital where I was working as a nurse; the train was as cold as a morgue, and you sat on your feet to keep them warm, and the carriages were stuffed with licentious soldiery. But London was not home; the country was, and 99 per cent of my childhood and adult life was spent there.

Then in 2003 I was widowed, after fifty-eight years of married life, every year of it spent living in the country. Nonetheless, after reflecting on all the practicalities, London became my new home. I found a house that seemed to have more of an air of a small country house than a town one. It looked west into a green space furnished with lawns, flowering shrubs and large trees. The front door was not on the street but opened on to a broad, private road bordered on either side by a four-foot wide pavement. This led into another private road, which ran along the back of my house and my neighbours' houses heading south. I had noticed on my inspection of the house a rather promising flat roof over the kitchen and ground-floor flat, which jutted out, running from west to east. It was on the level of the first floor. Ah, I thought: what about a roof garden here?

I bought two books by experts on creating roof gardens, but although they gave excellent advice on the practicalities of construction, irrigation, etc. – lots of decking, shiny white or bright red tiles for flooring and a good deal of wire, metal and steel – I could find little aesthetic inspiration.

Not surprisingly, my most grievous troubles and difficulties were with council and Health and Safety gurus. It seemed they did not smile on most of my ideas for making a beautiful 'garden in

the sky', though mine was not very high in the sky. Walls would collapse if I put trellis on them, they said, though I explained nobody could lean on the trellis because there were to be high and wide metal troughs full of climbers, bushy plants and soil. 'Someone might trip over the troughs and fall against the trellis' (and, I suppose, like Humpty Dumpty, have a great fall), taking wall and trellis with them into the road below. It was a frightening scenario, and the possibility couldn't be entertained. I silently wondered if I might be thought likely to have drunken elephants for summer parties on my roof. Against the low wall between me and my neighbour on the south, there was to be no trellis in case it gave all the neighbours ideas and they would copy it, surrounding their flat roofs with rose-and-honeysuckle-covered trellis like mine. I restrained myself from saying, 'Wouldn't it be rather nice if they did?' At last I passed the test, in spite of the squares in my trellis being larger than they allowed, 'which we are prepared to overlook'. I was sorely tempted to enquire what sort or kind of creature might fall through a square of 5 × 5 1/2 inches.

I wanted my roof garden to be a working one, so I have a small lean-to greenhouse, a potting bench, a wooden bower, the seat of which lifts up to reveal a box for tools and watering can, labels and tying wire, and another seat that does the same, eight wooden folding chairs, a table, a sun umbrella and a long chair for rest when work is done. There is also an auricula theatre for my beloved stage auriculas, impossibly beautiful in their perfection, which is, as Sacheverell Sitwell says, that of the most exquisite porcelain. I first saw the flower nearly fifty years ago, and fell in love with a passion that has never faded, and which I write about further on pages 198–201.

I had a bright idea for creating the beds for planting. I would collect from farmers galvanized iron cattle troughs they no longer needed in their fields, paint them as though they were lead, drill drainage holes in their bottoms and put in a good layer of drainage material and then a layer of well-rotted manure, followed by topsoil up to their rims, mixed with compost. The plants seem to thrive in them and I have four ten-footers and seven three-footers on the roof, and pots of various sizes and shapes packed with plants. As I sit in my drawing room or in my studio, I can look out, and in the spring, see the flowers of early roses and clematis so precious in London with its ten-degree higher temperature, the tulips, narcissus and the small jewel-like bulbs of *Iris histrioides*, and *I. reticulata*, and a tiny tulip, its snowy petals with steel-blue centres and sooty stamens treasures that can be missed in large gardens but are now under one's eye and can be studied in detail – one of the newly discovered pleasures of a roof garden. Every inch of soil is precious when planting is limited and there is such a multiplicity of 'must-have' plants.

Here is where climbers are so useful. They take up little ground space, but clothe the trellised walls and frame the archway over the gate of trellis that leads into the last third of the roof garden. The Health and Safety people said I must have this gate locked, and what's more with a bolt and a padlock on it in case anyone fell off the end of the roof; and I'm glad they did, as it creates a small, more secret space, and makes you want to discover what is going on behind. Part of what is going on behind is a line of four square painted tubs planted with olive trees (*Olea europaea*), their foliage mingling together and making a silvery wall. In January, the month I am writing this, my neighbour to the east has a *Prunus subhirtella* 'Autumnalis' in full flower, a cloud of palest pink; his garden is over the road and quite far away and I am grateful to him, for from my studio window it seems, with a little stretch of imagination, as though my garden continues into a wee wood or spinney, for he has other trees that play a part in the illusion.

I have another neighbour who has earned my gratitude as well. His house lies next door, and to the north of me. Its tall white-stuccoed wall rises up opposite my kitchen wing, which has the garden on its roof. I had already put troughs along the walls of the kitchen, at street level, one at the end of the wing and three under the windows either side of the back door facing north. My compost maker is there too. It looks like a beehive and I love it, not only for its looks but for the lovely stuff that comes out of it, largely thanks to the hundreds of little red worms working away in its inside. The plants are happy here, liking the cool root runs, the roses and climbers rushing up the brick walls and on to the trellis, when I have to shin up a ladder to tie them in. There is yellow double *Rosa banksiae*, thick with flowers

The Bower

in May, a dusty pink *Clematis* 'Hagley Hybrid', and the winter-flowering *Lonicera fragrantissima*, which I've found flowers better pruned against a wall. The *Pelargonium tomentosum*, peppermint scented, its leaves emerald-green velvet, developed into a huge bush hanging down the sides of the trough to the pavement below, and climbing four feet up the wall, liberated from its usual pot, it produced a mass of airy white flowers which were a revelation to me. And then there are lilies and lily of the valley, as well as a pair of round-headed box standards in lead pots on either side of the back door.

I wondered if my neighbour would let me put against his wall a water butt, a small wooden potting shed, two ten-foot-long cattle troughs, an assortment of low stone troughs of alpines, as well as a pair of Italian terracotta pots with standard bay trees in them, as well as panels of trellis ten feet wide and seven feet high, fixed to the back of the troughs. My kindly neighbour said he thought it would all look very nice. Agreeable things do happen every now and again and this was one of them.

In my dreams about what I would grow in my town garden, never in the wildest one did I imagine a trough full of vegetables, but there one day in June on my return from France was one of the troughs against my neighbour's wall, crowded with baby plants of lettuce, onions large and small, beetroot, parsnips, carrots and radishes, tomatoes starting up the trellis and runner beans likewise, while there was even a couple of courgette plants, and an aubergine shining in its amethyst skin. Here was another agreeable thing that happened and it came about through the kindness of one man who does the work of three, and who brought the little veggie plants up for me and planted them in the trough – a carpenter, painter, china restorer, gardener, a 'Jack of all trades' who in his work changes the last line from 'but master of none' to 'and master of all'. The trough next to the vegetables has a collection of herbs grown for one purpose only, to flavour the food, but nonetheless they please the eye as well with their quiet colours, and the nose with their scents.

As I prowl about my garden on the roof on a June evening when there is a moon, or when the soft lights come on as I move, while shadows deepen to a sooty black, emphasizing the faces of the flowers, and the sky above me is alive with stars, I can, for a moment eliminate from my consciousness the noise of the speed freaks roaring through the square and the cries of the yobs who have climbed into the square garden and are having a drunken party on the grass. There is even a twitter or two from some sleepy bird. One, almost, for a moment, might be in the country.

AN AURICULA THEATRE

THE NEW YORK BOTANICAL GARDEN

What do the Flemish weavers, Emperor Maximilian II, the monks at Tournai and Douai, Sir Thomas Hanmer, the weavers of Lancashire, the cutlers of Sheffield, Sacheverell Sitwell, Clusius, John Gerard, Parkinson, Hogg, Rea and Hyatt have in common? You might find it a puzzle to trace a link between these diverse characters and people, especially as they lived in five different centuries. Nonetheless, all of them shared a common interest to a lesser or greater degree: an admiration for, or an exceptional interest in – and in some cases a passion amounting to worship – for one particular plant, the auricula.

They discovered them, grew them, bred them, exchanged them, showed them, developed them or, in one way and another, had their lives or work, or both, influenced by their admiration and love for this plant, which was found growing in the mountain regions that extend from the Caucasus to the Pyrenees.

The plant was first introduced to England in 1580, most probably by the Flemish weavers as they fled from persecution. For several centuries, gardeners knew it as bear's ears, because of the form of its leaves, which gave it the name *Primula ursi* – though at that time the Emperor Maximilian's gardener, Clusius, called it *Sanicula alpina*. John Parkinson, a century later, gave it in his book *Paradisus al Sole* the delightful name of the French cowslip. He describes twenty-one varieties and illustrates eight, showing how the plant had advanced in popularity from a decade earlier when John Gerard, another botanist, described in his *Herbal* seven varieties, giving their colours. Sir Thomas Hanmer (that ardent supporter of Charles I) grew forty varieties of auricula in his garden in Wales, passing on several varieties to another enthusiast of much learning, a Dr John Rea, who grew an astonishing black-flowered plant named 'Black Imperial', which could have been the plant to have given the black ground colour to the edged varieties of a later date. The striped auricula and a double were both grown by Sir Thomas, only to vanish or anyway never to be recorded as established until their reappearance in modern times.

Hanmer is the first grower to mention the meal on an auricula plant. 'They have a larger whiter, mealier leaf than the purples have,' he writes of the ones he calls 'hair coloured'. It is not till 1728 that we read of anything further being recorded of changes in the form or characteristics of the flower. It is at that date that mention is made of a Dr Green's *Auricula ursi* with a truss of forty-five peeps (from which one supposes comes the modern word pips, meaning flowers – but peeps has the greater charm), 'a deep crimson colour with a white eye well powdered'.

Because of the powder, or meal, the auricula was now grown in pots indoors, for when the rain fell, the powder was spoiled. It would have certainly ruined the well-powdered plant raised by Dr Green and described in the minutes of the Spalding Gentleman's Society in 1728. By 1732, the auricula had developed to a high and refined standard. Besides the famous 'Black Imperial', another plant had appeared, its flower with a paste-like middle to it and covered all over with white powder. I suppose at this point there had arrived some likeness to today's white- and grey-edged auriculas, with their paste centres, black ground colour and petals covered with meal.

At this date, on the Continent, the auricula had become enormously popular and enthusiasts had begun to build 'theatres' for them. The monks at Tournai and Douai had a dozen of these theatres, with shelves arranged in tiers to show off their precious plants. The doubles, their colours described as sky blue, peach, pink and crimson, must have been astonishing beauties, as must two other plants, one striped in crimson and white, and the other in crimson and yellow. You can almost feel the excitement and admiration the sight of these plants caused their worshippers as they gazed at shelves laden with the newly created flowers that looked more like pieces of Meissen porcelain than something growing and alive.

But they were to become even more eye-popping with the arrival of the edged auricula in 1750. A flower appeared with a centre of thick white paste; its ground black and its edge green, or sometimes grey, which replaced the coloured petals with leaf characteristics, the centre's paste appearing also at the base of the leaves, which formed the calyx of the flower.

That this extraordinary flower had appeared wasn't so strange after all, for the ingredients that went to make it were already there with Dr Rea's 'Black Imperial' and Dr Green's 'powdered eye' and mealy flower. Many crossings were made with these plants and, as Roy Genders says, 'the structural transformation of the petals took place and the edged auricula was born'. The first named variety was called 'Rule Arbiter'. It was introduced in 1757 and auriculas became at once extremely popular, especially amongst the weavers of Yorkshire and Lancashire; sometimes as many as fifty auricula shows were held each year in the

north of England, Manchester and Sheffield being the most important centres to hold them. This dramatic development in the auricula plant took place at the turn of the nineteenth century and fifty years later the show auricula had reached a state of perfection never surpassed, or so claim the old growers. To the weavers of Lancashire and Cheshire, and the cutlers of Sheffield, belongs the explanation for the quality the auricula had by this time attained. As descendants of the Flemish weavers, they had had handed down to them a vast knowledge of how to cultivate the plant, and they were self-employed, which meant that when their work was done they could give the kind of attention the plants needed if they were to reach perfection.

There has, I think, been something of a renaissance in the world of stage auriculas in the last few years, but it is as yet limited. Sadly, modern life leaves little time for the meticulous attention they need. A hundred and fifty years ago, there were few distractions to rival the exquisite pleasure of growing the auricula.

If you want to live a long life, become an auricula grower, for growers seem to flourish (as did their plants), living into their late eighties and even nineties. It is no legend that they were the longest lived of all the people in the nineteenth century – their lives prolonged perhaps by work, interest, love and beauty plus the spice of competition and hope, always the hope that your most brilliant plants were going to be even better next year – you had to go on living to see them.

Many of the names of nineteenth-century auricula growers are remembered by today's enthusiasts, Hogg, Glenning and Maddock among them. One, Emmerton, lived in Barnet, near Hatfield, and published his *Treatise of the Culture and Management of the Auricula*, which he dedicated to one of my predecessors, the 2nd Marchioness of Salisbury, but there are no records to show that she ever grew them. They are plants that need the dedicated attention of a lover, and the huge gardens and hothouses of a country house with its pack of gardeners under a head is not an environment where they would find a place.

I began growing them at the manor at Cranborne, having fallen utterly in love with them at first sight. My feelings are those of Sacheverell Sitwell when he first saw them. I quote his words;

The first time I beheld a stage auricula – it was hardly to be conceived possible that such a plant should exist at all. There is something improbable in its edging and mealing. This latter has been stippled or dappled on to it. The white mealy eye of the flower is a glorious and wonderful thing; but the slight and miraculous powdering upon the back of the flower is even more striking. Then the meal upon the leaves of the plant is an aesthetic and even sensual pleasure of the highest order . . .

This first moment of seeing a stage auricula is an experience never to be forgotten. It would seem incredible that a flower through human skill should attain to this degree of natural or trained artificiality, for the perfection of a stage auricula is that of the most exquisite Meissen porcelain [or] of the most lovely silk stuffs of Isfahan, which is to say that it attains to the highest technical standards of human craftsmanship. And yet it is a living and growing thing with the gift of procreation . . .

It might be argued that a fine stage auricula is among the most beautiful things in nature or in the world of human beings . . .nature does not necessarily . . . mean a wild and uncontrolled growth, a picturesque confusion. For the auricula epitomises nature controlled and in the service of man. It belongs to epochs of discipline and order to the day of living architecture and the law of life.

The effect of this flower is to be compared to that slight disintegration of the senses when features or limbs of a ravishing loveliness are seen. A perfection of physical beauty produces this bewilderment and wonder. . . . It must be looked at in silence; for fear that it should vanish. And then the humanity of this flower dawns in comfort upon the mind; and this is to be compared to the voice, or to the expression in the eyes of that human vision, which now reveals itself to be growing from the soil.

When, after my father-in-law's death, we moved to Hatfield, I took the small greenhouse where I grew my stage auriculas and set it up in the place where I designed a few years later the new kitchen garden. What exquisite pleasure they gave each year in the weeks of April and May when they were in flower! I joined the Auricula Society and looked forward each year to the displays at Chelsea and the Royal Horticultural Society shows in London, and new plants were added to my collection.

Brenda Hyatt became my friend, one of the greatest of the modern growers, and I was very touched when she gave my name to a plant she had bred and let me choose which it should be. A martyr to asthma, Brenda died before she was old (an exception perhaps to prove the rule for auricula growers), leaving me her collection. Her death was a sad loss to all her many friends and to the world of auriculas.

Some years later, I had a small auricula theatre made and hung it on the east wall of one of the garden houses on the south front of the house at Hatfield. It was in painted wood with a proscenium arch and side curtains. The curtains were dark green with tiebacks and braided in deep yellow. The dark tobacco-brown interior was a good background to show off the trusses, and their pots sat on shelves inside. I now have it fixed on a panel of the trellis which surrounds my roof garden in London, described on page 194.

It was this theatre that Gregory Long, the President of the New York Botanical Garden, saw when he brought a party of friends from the garden to visit Hatfield before my husband's death, and later he asked me if I would design an auricula theatre for the Botanical Garden. It was a commission after my own heart. As, at that time, the garden had no stage auriculas. I sent them catalogues and information, so they could begin to build a collection, from which the best plants could be chosen to decorate the theatre. This was to be ready for an opening in April 2007. On a visit to America in 2006 for design jobs in Connecticut and New York, I met Gregory Long and Todd Forrest, Director of the Botanical Garden, to choose the site for the theatre. I very much liked the suggested place, in the charming walled garden designed and planted some years ago by Penelope Hobhouse. Here were many of the plants and bulbs that would have been grown when the vogue for auricula theatres was at its peak. The theatre was to be fixed against the brick wall of the garden, facing north, which is the aspect preferred by the plants. It was so arranged that when the flowering season was over, about the second week in May, the theatre could be removed.

Todd Forrest took on the job of supervising the creation of the theatre itself. When I was making my theatre at Hatfield I had discovered, at Lord Leicester's estate at Holkham in Norfolk, a paint for outdoor use that not only offered colours that worked well with the tones found in plants and trees, but also had the advantage of lasting longer than other outdoor paints. We chose a colour from this range. Christianson Lee, an expert in both woodwork and painting, made an excellent job of constructing and colouring the theatre.

Meanwhile, part of the glorious new glasshouse was for some weeks full of stage auriculas – thousands of them – I had never seen so many together in my life before, all looked after with tender loving care by Marc Hachodoenion and Sharita Mason. With such an embarrassment of riches the task of keeping the theatre furnished with plants in their prime from late April to early May could not be a difficult one.

On 26 April 2007 all was ready for the opening. There was a ribbon to be cut, a crowd, the press, and the sun came out.

INDEX

Entries in *italics* refer to illustrations.

ACKNOWLEDGEMENTS

Author's Acknowledgements

I would like to thank the many people who have supported me in so many ways in writing this book. Importantly, Derry Moore, who took the superb photographs and who has been a perfect delight to work with, as he was when we collaborated on my first book on *The Gardens of Queen Elizabeth, the Queen Mother*; John Nicoll, my publisher, for encouraging me to write this book; Jo Christian, my editor, who has been unfailingly helpful, patient and encouraging in times when I lost confidence in what I was doing; Anne Askwith, who edited my text so skilfully; Becky Clarke, for her beautiful book design; and my tireless secretary, Elizabeth Dean, so clever and adroit in deciphering the messy pages I gave to her, and in swiftly converting them into readable form on the computer. To all of them I am deeply grateful.

Acknowledgements for the Photographs and Drawings

All photographs copyright © Derry Moore except for those on the following pages:
pages 11, 15, 16, 17, 30, 167, collection of the Dowager Marchioness of Salisbury;
page 48, courtesy of Lord and Lady Brabourne;
page 126, courtesy of Alec Cobbe;
page 165, courtesy of Il Duca and La Duchessa Salviati;
pages 188 and 190, courtesy of the Museum of Garden History.

All drawings copyright © The Dowager Marchioness of Salisbury, except for the plan on page 86, courtesy of The Marquess of Salisbury.